Behind
the
Seams

For fans of *The Great British Sewing Bee*:

The Great British Sewing Bee: Sustainable Style
by Alexandra Bruce and Caroline Akselson

*The Great British Sewing Bee: The Modern Wardrobe
(Create the Clothes You Love with 28 Projects and
Innovative Alteration Techniques)* by Juliet Uzor

Behind the Seams

Esme Young

My life in creativity, friendship and adventure

BLINK
bringing you closer

First published in the UK by Blink Publishing
An imprint of Bonnier Books UK
4th Floor, Victoria House,
Bloomsbury Square, London,
WC1B 4DA

Owned by Bonnier Books
Sveavägen 56, Stockholm, Sweden

Hardback – 978-1-788704-62-5
Ebook – 978-1-788704-63-2
Audio – 978-1-788704-64-9

A CIP catalogue of this book is available from the British Library.

Designed by Envy Design Ltd
Printed and bound by Clays Ltd, Elcograf S.p.A

1 3 5 7 9 10 8 6 4 2

Blink Publishing is an imprint of Bonnier Books UK
www.bonnierbooks.co.uk

With love to my siblings; Fiona, Christopher, Angus and Jeremy

Contents

CHAPTER 1

Daydream Believer

I feel I should begin at the beginning, although I'm not sure it is always the best place to start. I rather like the idea of going backwards and getting younger with each chapter but then I have always looked at things from a different perspective. There is something so pleasing about going against expectation and convention, finding your own way. For the most part it's been a successful approach throughout my life and career, apart from those times when it hasn't, but more of that later.

You may have this book because you know me from the BBC's *The Great British Sewing Bee*, which is another reason why I could begin my story at the end. The truth is it's just one exciting part of a much bigger, interesting tale that explains how I ended up on the nation's TV screens, so I may as well start from the moment the stork delivered me one cold, miserable February day in 1949 in Bedford ...

I arrived and immediately interrupted the peace for my older sister Fiona, who, until then, had been perfectly happy being the perfectly well-behaved only child. I also upset my mum. She suffered with postnatal depression after my birth and possibly after the birth of my brothers, Christopher, Angus and Jeremy. I only discovered this much later but the knowledge of her struggle made sense of some things in my childhood and gave me a clearer perspective of her as a woman and mother. She was great fun but far from easy.

In those days postnatal depression was referred to somewhat dismissively as the 'baby blues' and there was little medical help or understanding. Instead new mothers were often left to get on with it and relied on their supportive family network, if they were lucky enough to have one. Thankfully my mum had two sisters who were able to help out. I was sent to live with Aunt Queenie for a few months when I was a tiny baby, which gave Mum a chance to recuperate. We always had 'the nanny' or 'the girl' too (which was much more common in those days) – a succession of helpful women of varying ages and qualifications who looked after us as we grew in raucous, rebellious number.

My mum's other sister, Aunt Sheila, would give up work for a while to look after each of my siblings as they arrived and we all grew incredibly fond of her and very much looked forward to her visits. Sheila's passion was for the theatre. She was by nature rather theatrical and quite eccentric, although in a completely unaffected way. She appeared on the stage in several productions, but given the life of an actor is so insecure and income uncertain, like so many others in that profession she 'fell back on' a more reliable employment. She earned her bread and butter as a secretary, working for various organisations, including a stint for the editor of the *Manchester Guardian* and in Strasbourg for the Council of Europe.

She was the kind of person who managed effortlessly to generate all sorts of dramas in her wake and when we were children, Mum loved to direct us in re-staging her more notorious escapades. Year after year at Christmas these re-enactments would have Mum hooting with laughter – the goings-on at Doncaster station in 1954 being a particular favourite. Aunt Sheila had been to stay and was catching the train from Doncaster to go home. We were all lined up on the platform to see her off and she was very theatrically bending down to kiss us all goodbye, one by one. As she swooped down on my brother Angus, who was about two years old at the time, there was a shrill blast on a whistle, Sheila shrieked in alarm and leapt aboard her train, only to discover the whistle was for a completely different train on another platform. She simply couldn't be coaxed back onto the platform to complete her fond farewells – I don't think Angus ever quite recovered.

When it was Sheila's 80th birthday we rented a farmhouse in the countryside near her home in Strasbourg and hosted a celebration for her. She was very touched to be made such a fuss of and to be reminded that we had not forgotten her, despite her being rather far away. She had been such a big part of our childhood and the truth was that we all loved her a very great deal.

My parents had five children in all. Fiona was the first and then me. Christopher, the unconventional one, came a few years after, quickly followed by Angus, the wild child, then four years later, Mum gave birth for the final time to Jeremy, the baby of the family. When the midwife announced, 'It's a lovely baby boy,' my mum said, 'Oh no, not another one!' as Christopher and Angus, being close in age, tended to fight and were quite a handful. This prompted the nurses to be concerned for my mum's mental health and they kept an eye on her.

One time, when Mum went to the bathroom, on seeing an empty bed, the nurses thought she had taken Jeremy with her and they were worried she was going to drown him or flush him down the loo. In fact, she had made a cocoon of blankets on the bed and left him safely swaddled inside and in their haste they hadn't noticed that. Her retort of 'How ridiculous!' didn't do much to appease them.

While my mum struggled to show her true feelings, my dad, Brian Young, expressed his love for us through his kind actions and thought for us all. Born in South Africa, to a British mum and South African dad, he was educated at the prestigious Michaelhouse school and was fluent in English, Afrikaans and Zulu. My grandfather, Kenneth Young, was a solicitor and was keen for Brian to follow his footsteps in to law but my dad had other ideas. Most Sundays, he would join his sister's boyfriend on his paper round, albeit one with a difference. Due to the vast spaces and remoteness of the terrain, the delivery would be made by aeroplane and my dad's job was to sling the newspapers out as they flew low over the properties. Occasionally he would be allowed to take the controls and this sparked a passion that would define his future.

Such was this passion for flying, he sat for and won a scholarship to the distinguished RAF College, Cranwell in Lincolnshire. While my grandfather had been doubtful about him taking up his place at Cranwell, my grandmother, Flora, felt that as a war in Europe was clearly coming and given that my dad would inevitably join up, it was better that he be properly trained and ready. She won the argument and so, instead of studying law, he got the approval he needed to accept his place on the two-year course. In August 1936, at the age of 18, setting sail from Durban aboard the RMS Llandovery Castle he was striking out on his own and becoming a young man. As the ship cut through the waters of the Indian Ocean towards the Suez Canal, taking him to England for the very first time, his life's journey was truly underway. And as things would turn out, he would never see his mum again.

While a cadet at Cranwell, my dad wrote a poem called *Flight* (which has been published in poetry anthologies and journals) that captured his love of flying:

How can they know the joy to be alive
    Who have not flown?
To loop and spin and roll and climb and dive,
    The very sky one's own,

The urge of power while engines race,
    The sting of speed,
The rude winds' buffet on one's face,
    To live indeed.

How can they know the grandeur of the sky,
    The earth below,
The restless sea, and waves that break and die
    With ceaseless ebb and flow;
The morning sun on drifting clouds
    And rolling downs –
And valley mist that shrouds
    The chimneyed towns?

So long has puny man to earth been chained
    Who now is free,
And with the conquest of the air has gained
    A glorious liberty.
How splendid is this gift He gave
    On high to roam,
The sun a friend, the earth a slave,
    The heavens home.

On graduating, from Cranwell in July 1938, he was awarded the title of Most Outstanding Cadet and the Sword of Honour – I imagine that recognition would have assuaged any lingering family tension! My dad was now commissioned into the Royal Air Force as a Pilot Officer joining 32 Squadron at Biggin Hill. One day, he was on duty in the signals room when a request came in asking his squadron to send a pilot to join 615 'Churchill's Own' squadron supporting the British Expeditionary Force in France. He was all alone so, without getting permission from the squadron commander, he replied, giving his own name, and a few weeks later, he was on his way to war, arriving in France with his squadron in November 1939. This might sound the very opposite of luck but this was exactly like my dad, to want to be where it mattered.

With all the confidence and belief of youth, he flew straight into the Battle of France in a Hurricane fighter plane. Sadly, he didn't last all that long. He was shot down over Belgium in May 1940 in a hail of bullets from a Messerschmitt 109 – the fuel tank in the hurricane caught fire immediately and my dad was badly burned. He managed to escape, remembering to dive forward out of the plane to avoid the tail plane, and dropped into a cloud, not opening his parachute until he was below it. Then he watched in shock as his aircraft crashed to the ground, luckily causing very little damage other than blowing a few tiles off a shed roof.

Fortunately, he came down behind the British front lines, but less fortunately, the British soldiers were a bit trigger-happy and, thinking he was a German pilot, put one bullet through his arm and two through his leg as he came down on his parachute. When he landed, they threw a grenade at him, exploding a hole in the side of his body. He was very seriously injured, losing consciousness, and almost naked apart from his boots (due to his clothes having been burned off), but he was also furious at being mistaken for a German pilot and he shouted at them. Realising their mistake, the soldiers were horrified: 'What have we done? We've shot an Englishman!' they wailed. True to form, my dad, despite his terrible wounds, said, 'I'm not a bloody Englishman, I'm a South African!' Unfortunately, he said it in Afrikaans, which to the British infantryman standing over him probably sounded a lot like German.

Incredibly, one of the men there that day was also South African and replied to him in Afrikaans. A medical student at Guy's Hospital when the war broke out, he had joined the Royal Army Medical Corps (RAMC). He just happened to be driving past in an ambulance. After convincing the soldiers that dad wasn't a German, but an RAF pilot, he immediately tended to the hole in my dad's side made by the grenade and this undoubtedly saved his life. He drove him to a casualty station where another amazing stroke of luck occurred.

As my dad lay in bed with third-degree burns covering his face and hands, and a wound running from his waist to his armpit, a doctor doing the rounds came up: 'Brian Young, you're a South African, aren't you?'

'Yes,' he replied.

'Are you related to Betty Young?' he asked.

'Yes, that's my sister!'

It turned out the doctor had been going out with Betty,

who was then in Edinburgh. More importantly, he gave my dad a crucial piece of advice: 'Your hands are quite badly burned, but you must keep flexing your fingers, however much it hurts. If you don't, the scar tissue will turn your hands into claws and they will be quite useless.' My dad was a determined man, as you can see, so he flexed his hands all the time, however painful and uncomfortable it was.

His adventures were not over yet though. After a few weeks being moved from one field hospital to another, he arrived in Normandy, where he was put in yet another ambulance and despatched to Cherbourg, with five other casualties, ready to be sent back to a hospital in England. As they arrived at the French port there was an air raid and the ambulance weaved around town, trying to avoid being hit. My dad was the first to fall out of his bunk and the rest followed, one by one, falling on top of him. When the driver opened the ambulance doors, his cargo of patients were all on the floor. My dad was at the very bottom of the pile and the only one who was still alive. Luckily for him (and for me as I wouldn't exist otherwise), he escaped death yet again. While in France he had continued writing poetry and while he had managed to survive his shooting down, in the chaos following it leading up to the Dunkirk evacuation, his poetry did not and was lost forever.

He eventually made it to a British military hospital in East Grinstead, specialising in reconstructive surgery for badly burned or crushed servicemen and known for its holistic approach to healing. There, he was treated by Sir Harold Gillies, one of the foremost experts of the time. On examining my dad, Gillies said, 'This may seem a silly question, but were your hands burned at the same time as the rest of your body?'

'Of course,' he replied.

'Then why are your hands still raw, while the rest of your burns have scar tissue?'

My dad raised his hands and, flexing his fingers, explained what he had been told to do.

'You are a very lucky young man to have received that advice,' he was informed.

My dad remained there for two years and recovered the use of his hands, which Harold Gillies called 'the miracle'. While there, he grew stronger, his wounds began to heal and his sense of humour bounced back too, although it was never far away even in his darkest moments. He could be terribly mischievous, as could my mum, something I think my siblings and I have inherited from them. He was known for keeping the other patients' spirits up, which must have been a welcome diversion from the pain, routine and boredom of a long hospital stay.

Just before one of my dad's operations the strict matron had told him he must be nil by mouth. Perturbed at the thought of not being able to eat, he asked the nurses if eating before the op would be bad for him. They told him it was Matron's rule only because she didn't want patients being sick on her so he ignored it and ate something. When he came round, he asked if he had vomited and they said gleefully, 'Oh yes! Everywhere!'

While he was there, he met two women. The first was Lady Esme Greene, a local aristocrat who lent horses to the patients as part of their convalescence. My dad once rode a horse up the steps and into the hospital before getting caught by his furious surgeon, who told him, 'One fall, one stray hoof and all the hard work on repairing your face will be gone.' He didn't ride into the hospital again but he never forgot the kindness of Lady Esme, who rode side saddle in a smart top hat.

The second woman was my mum, Patricia Cole, who had entered nursing to help with the war effort and worked at the hospital. She was young, glamorous and full of life and she caught my dad's eye. But it took him a while to persuade her to go out with him after he had sworn at her when she accidentally pulled off some grafted skin while giving him a bed bath, but as usual, he persevered.

It is easy to tell the story of my brave, dashing dad – particularly as some of it is documented in the Imperial War Museum archives. My mum is much more complicated to pin down. She was the product of a difficult upbringing – my grandfather, Thomas Cole, had a Victorian approach to parenting and was incredibly strict and cold towards her. He was a senior officer in the Royal Irish Constabulary (RIC) and as such, employed by the British Government. After the Easter Rising in Dublin of 1916 and the subsequent war for Irish Independence, he was part of the British effort to suppress the Irish struggle to achieve independence. He was therefore regarded as a traitor by the IRA (Irish Republican Army) and sentenced to death in absentia. As the authority of the British Government collapsed progressively from 1920 onwards and the position of RIC officers became increasingly dangerous, he was relocated to England following the Anglo-Irish Treaty of 1921. Even though he was now living in Bedford, he knew that he might still be a target for the IRA and indeed many years later, there was a knock at the door. My grandfather opened it to a man that he knew to be from the IRA: 'Have you come to get me, Paddy?' he asked. Fortunately, Paddy had come to reminisce over a cup of tea and was seeking reconciliation, not retribution.

Although my mum was born in Ireland, of Irish parentage, because of this history, she only spent the first few months of her life there and always regarded herself as English.

Mum was a talented diver, so much so that she was asked to join the Olympic diving team, but my grandfather forbade it. When my dad proposed to my mum he asked my grandfather for his consent and the response was, 'Brian, she isn't good enough for you.' I can't begin to imagine how Mum must have felt but I think the way she was parented informed her relationship with her own children – she struggled to show us emotion and be loving towards us. That's not to say she wasn't great company

– in fact, what she lacked in showing affection, she made up for in laughs. She loved a prank, particularly if she was the one who was playing them and she often did, much to Dad's bewilderment. He had a good sense of humour but he didn't understand my mum's fondness for practical jokes. They included capers like making 'apple pie' beds (where the sheet is folded in half so you can't stretch your legs out), ambushing us as we left the house by throwing water bombs out of the bedroom window and leaving eggs in Mr McNally, the gardener's, umbrella. Once, she wrote a letter to my grandmother pretending to be the explorer Edmund Hillary's secretary and inviting her to join his next expedition to Mount Everest, citing her as the ideal candidate.

As children we often benefited from her alternative approach to life and the ease with which she slipped into role play, or imaginary worlds that she invited us into. When Angus was little and we were living in France, she created a fictional character called Gertrude, who would visit him while he was sleeping. My mum and sister Fiona would buy plastic rings from Prisunic, the French version of Woolworths, and Gertrude left them for Angus overnight, so when he woke up, he was bejewelled like an Emperor. 'Gertrude' would pen little messages of endearment on brown parcel labels and tie them to the plastic ring on his finger. This both bemused and pleased Angus, who was desperate for our mum's attention. Once when he was a teenager, she encouraged him to dress up in an outlandish outfit – he wore rugby boots, Dad's huge rugby socks, an Express Dairy milkman's coat, chiffon scarf and dark bug-eyed sunglasses with a cane. He joined the queue at the fish and chip shop while Mum watched gleefully from the car, roaring with laughter. Perhaps it was this sort of escapade that sparked his interest in acting? Or perhaps he was inspired by Aunt Sheila – because he subsequently trained as an actor at the Webber Douglas Academy of Dramatic Art and has appeared on stage and played parts on TV and in films.

Mum loved the slapstick humour of the *Carry On* films and would take us all to the cinema regularly. She adored parties and dressing up too, which was lucky considering the amount of entertaining that came with Dad's job. Rake-thin, she looked fabulous in anything – I think how she dressed (and the *Vogue*, *Queen* and *Harper's Bazaar* magazines that arrived monthly) ignited my lifelong love of clothes and I would make the occasional outfit for her and fancy dress costumes. She was a free spirit, a tricky thing to be in those days, and this also confused my dad.

Dad's job in the RAF not only meant us moving as a family every couple of years, but he also had to travel a lot and regularly left my mum behind in strange new places. When I was born, over seven years after they met, he had just returned from the Middle East. My mum wanted to call me Caroline but Dad was adamant that I should be named Esme, after his kind horsewoman. He had been away working when my sister was born and had not named her so this time he got his way, much to the annoyance of Mum, who refused to call me Esme. Instead, I was called Emma and answered to that name until I was 18 and went away to college. On my first morning at St Martins the tutor took the register and called out 'Esme Young', having taken my name from the formal application. I put my hand up and said that was the name on my birth certificate but I was known as Emma. He looked startled and then frowned. 'Why on earth would you change your name from Esme to Emma?' he asked. 'Esme is such a lovely name.' He then quoted from his favourite book, JD Salinger's *For Esme – with Love and Squalor*. I became Esme immediately.

But I have just jumped forward 18 years and I'm getting ahead of myself.

⊗ ⊗ ⊗

My earliest memories lie in Bawtry in South Yorkshire. I was about three years old when Dad was stationed there, and in my short life I had already lived in Bedford and then Hemswell in Lincolnshire. I have flashes of images during this time. Like being in the car with Dad, where I would thrust my feet on the front seat of the car while he encouraged me, 'Push! Push!' and I would believe I was pushing the car up the hill. Or me standing on tiptoes outside my parents' friends' house, nose pressed against the window, trying to catch a glimpse of the Queen's Coronation on their brand-new bulky television set. My mum was inside, but no children were allowed as they might fidget and ruin the viewing experience. I was a very sociable child and was often visiting other families on the RAF base. It was also the best way to score biscuits and there was one house that I would regularly knock on the door of as they would also have bowls of crisps out in the sitting room. I would sneak off and grab a handful while nobody was looking until the time the woman, wise to my tactics, hid behind the sofa and jumped out on me. It gave me such a shock and I never went back.

As a small child I was in a world of my own and it was a very beautiful place to be. I spent most of my time happily creating things; paintings and drawings as well as crafting little grass and flower houses for fairies. When I was four, I remember being very proud of a picture I drew of a pirate ship complete with Captain Hook. I was obsessed with art and the more I did, the better I became. What my parents didn't realise – and I was too young to understand – was the other reason for my creative focus. It was an escape from the real world, a confusing place which I struggled to understand because I couldn't hear for I was partially deaf. We didn't know this at the time.

At the age of five, I was sent off to boarding school. We were sent away – the girls to one school and the two older boys to another – with varying degrees of dread and loathing. I remember being dropped off by my parents and begging them not to leave me. I appeared to be incredibly upset, and I know I certainly wasn't happy, but I also remember a feeling of fraudulence, of not being quite as sad as I should be. Maybe I was too young to realise exactly what it meant or maybe I reacted to all the other girls around me, who were making a jolly good show of devastation by sobbing and clinging to their parents. The reality was my older sister Fiona was already there, Mum wasn't the cosy type and Dad was away a lot. I settled pretty quickly and the older girls spoilt me in my first year.

My school was the Convent of the Holy Ghost in Bedford – the same school my mum had been to – and we were taught by nuns, part of a French order that had resettled in Bedford some 50 years earlier. They were mostly excellent teachers and had created a surprisingly forward-thinking environment. Any concerns about us being encouraged to give our lives to God and follow them into the Order were unfounded and there were strict rules against indoctrination. On one occasion a member of domestic staff was a little too zealous and she was immediately sent packing.

Our school boarding house was just out of town. Built in 1872, it was an imposing red brick gothic-style mansion, more suited as a backdrop to old horror films than a home for young girls who were missing their families. Set in leafy Clapham Park, it boasted the 'finest views in the Midlands extending into five counties'. What it didn't boast in those days was any functional heating and even in a dormitory crammed with girls, we had to get dressed in bed under our blankets. It was the only lingering warmth to be found in the morning.

We were taken into Bedford each day for school and then returned in time for supper – the food was very good and there were always bowls of raw carrots for snacks. On a Sunday after church we were given thick slices of buttered white bread and a bar of chocolate. We would break the chocolate into crumbs on top of the bread to make deliciously sweet sandwiches. Then we each wrote a letter home but there was no hope for an honest account or any soul baring because the nuns read them before they were sent and we were scared we would get into trouble. My letters would mostly look like this:

Dear Mum and Dad,
How are you?
I have been playing hockey.
Love Emma

When I was young, I was quite sporty. As well as hockey, I was in the netball team and played goal defence, and I was the school high jump champion. That may come as a surprise as I am quite small, but I was bigger then – compared to the other children, that is. I grew early then stopped in my early teens, so they all overtook me. Even so it's quite a funny idea that I was a high jumper.

I tried to run away several times. I would wait for everyone to be asleep, dress silently and creep down the wide oak staircase, letting myself out of the unlocked front door. There was a long drive that led directly away from the house and I ran down it, bolstered by my own bravado, trying not to be scared by the darkness and strange nocturnal noises. I didn't know this at the time but the drive was around two miles long. I never reached the main road. There was always a moment when I realised it was an awfully long way and I was really rather tired. I never considered what I would do once I got to the main gate and had no idea where to go so I would turn and run back, letting myself quietly into the house, creeping up the stairs and managing to get back into bed without anyone knowing I had gone. I think I escaped just because I could and not because I wanted to leave school. The moonlit flit was my little secret and it was thrilling to do it without ever getting caught.

In the first couple of years of my school life the teachers raised concerns about my ability to concentrate in lessons and understand what I was being taught. I don't think they said it as politely as that, I think they called me stupid. My dad dismissed this crossly, saying I was just a bit 'dreamy'. At the same time, one of the nuns was doing a course on dyslexia (which must have been progressive for a convent school in the mid-1950s) and it was decided I would be her case study. She gave me a notebook and asked me to write in it. I can't remember what I was supposed to be writing about, but I didn't put one word down. Instead, I filled it with drawings including a stylised way of sketching flowers and pictures inspired by the Impressionists – it was the best way I knew of expressing myself and I don't think I wanted to be judged by her.

I found an old photo of me recently, taken when I was in the Brownies, surrounded by other girls from my pack. We were sitting cross-legged in full uniform with jaunty berets, neatly tied cravats and leather belts cinched at the waist. Everyone is looking at the camera and the photographer must have asked us to 'Smile, please' or said something funny because all the girls are grinning and laughing. Everyone that is except for me. Adult me stared at the picture wondering what on earth had made child me look so serious and then I realised I wouldn't have heard the photographer. I would have had no idea when the photo would be taken, the joke that had just been relayed or that I had been asked to look happy.

By the time I was seven, I was sent to the doctor. The nuns and my parents must have had an inkling there was something else behind my 'dreaminess' or 'stupidity'. It was then they discovered I was partially deaf due to something known as 'glue ear', where there is a build-up of fluid in the ear canal. My case was particularly severe so I had my tonsils and adenoids removed to rectify it. It was just in time because my early learning was becoming seriously affected – I had been unable to read as I couldn't learn the words phonetically and had to recognise them as spellings. Once I started to read, I couldn't stop. I don't know if my early academic struggle was due to my deafness or dyslexia but I would guess it was the former although I continued to believe I was dyslexic for many years. The silver lining to this experience was finding refuge in my sketchbooks, pencils and paints and the joy I discovered there. Maybe without this temporary disability my life might have turned out differently but I'm very glad it didn't.

All my teachers were passionate about their subjects, which made learning so much easier, and I loved lessons about Greek culture and history of art especially – it was one of my history of art teachers who saw my potential and encouraged me to keep drawing. And another, the daughter of a trade union boss, who liked impressionism, took us all to the National Gallery to look at Post-Impressionist paintings by Paul Cézanne, a memory that still shines brightly. Often we were taken on day trips to expand our minds. Every afternoon, Sister Mary Magdalene read to us, the sort of children's fiction we were desperate for her to read one more chapter of before she closed the book. We would perform little shows for the nuns and they laughed uproariously at my impersonation of Cliff Richard singing 'Living Doll'.

My school uniform was navy – V-neck tunic, flared skirt, smart blazer – and white shirt and blue-and-white striped tie. There were regulation sandals for summer and stout lace-up shoes in winter. None of us could ever wear the uniform as it was supposed to be; there were ways to surreptitiously adapt it, whether with a loose tie, one sock ruffled at the ankle or the waistband of the skirt turned over to raise the hem slightly. Every Friday the laundry came back and we would have to mend our uniforms and socks. This was how I learnt to sew and darn as well as knit and crochet, skills that were to become the tools of my trade many years later. I was seven when I made my first garment, a gathered skirt.

Going home for the holidays held the biggest excitement for me. There was always a level of jeopardy about whether I would be picked up because Mum was absent-minded and had forgotten each of us at different times. Once, I was sitting in the dormitory with all the other girls, bags packed and noise levels at their highest. One by one they were collected, throwing out cheery goodbyes as they skipped away. No one wanted to be the last to go and as the day wore on, I had a sinking feeling it would be me. And then worse, that my parents weren't coming at all.

The nuns phoned home and I remained at school for another night and the precious start of the holiday. I ate dinner alone at one of the big refectory tables and slept in an eerily silent dorm before Dad raced over in the morning full of apologies. I think that was a rare occurrence but it has stayed with me. So too have all the wonderful times when Fiona and I were collected by our dad. We would sing songs in the car, going through the alphabet until he shouted 'STOP!' and whichever letter we were on prompted the title of the next song, like a funny little human jukebox. I loved those journeys, speeding to wherever home was and stopping to buy fish and chips on the way – a favourite ritual.

I couldn't wait to be reunited with all my siblings and we revelled in high jinks and adventure. We also fought and bickered too but no more than you would expect from five children, away at school for long periods of time, who were growing rapidly and developing their own strong characters. Fiona was sensible and managed to separate herself from any bad behaviour and Jeremy was the littlest so he didn't count for a few years. It was me, Christopher and Angus who were the best of friends and a happy gang, although it took years for Chris to accept his younger brother after Angus' arrival usurped him as the baby of the family. When he was a teenager he announced to our mum that he was hatching the perfect murder with Angus as the victim. He just made it up to be provocative of course, but it was an indication of the continuing tensions between them. Interestingly, he and Angus bonded when they were teenagers and are still very close today.

In one photo I have of us, we are standing in a line, next to Aunt Betty. I'm about eight and have a big plaster on my knee – typical of me as I ran full pelt everywhere and was constantly falling over. I'm smiling straight at the camera with my hands in my jacket pockets. Christopher, at the other end of the line, is about six years old, in smart shorts, jumper and shirt, hands clasped formally in front of him. He has a serious expression almost tipping into a frown. In the middle of the line, in a zip-up cardigan and shorts with scuffed shoes, is Angus, whose little face is creased into such infectious delight. His cheekiness and spirit for life bursts out of the photograph and when I look at it now, I'm transported straight back to that time.

For several years, when we were young, summer holidays involved a trip to Scotland to visit Aunt Betty and Uncle Hamish in Edinburgh. Uncle Hamish was quite a character. He was a lawyer, but was also an expert on rhododendrons and had a lot of them in his garden. However, he found that the demands of his legal career left him little time to tend to them, particularly in winter when the days were short, so he had floodlights installed and used to garden at night, with a traditional-style editor's green visor on. He had an old Lagonda car, which he had decided he would dismantle and put back together, but halfway through, he got bored, so he greased all the parts to avoid rust, then left it dismantled in the garage.

A descendant of David Hume, the philosopher, he had a portrait of Hume in the dining room. My brother Jeremy asked him how much it cost to insure and he glibly replied that the insurance was too expensive, so he hadn't got any. He also told us that we shouldn't go into the dining room at night as it was protected by a laser alarm system. When he died, the picture went to the National Gallery of Scotland.

Mum had nicknames for each of us when we were little and they changed as we grew older and no longer suited the baby names. Jeremy, the youngest, was Big Boy Bubba, although we think he may have originally been Clooty Clucker. When Chris was a toddler, he was called Ollie Hardy after the chubby actor in the legendary entertainment duo Laurel and Hardy, before being known as Kiddy Muncher. I was Emma Bobsie, Angus was Gaga and we can't remember Fiona's name but she must have had one.

In the holidays, we had lots of freedom outdoors – a relief after boarding school and the enforced weekend walks, which sometimes led past my grandmother Mary's grave. At home we were free to roam the countryside without adult supervision, making dens, playing games and foraging for hazelnuts and blackberries. We all loved being immersed in nature even if I did take it too far occasionally. I discovered a dead rat in a field and thought it would be fun to chase Chris with it. He screamed in terror and raced ahead of me as I whirled it around my head by its tail until the tail became detached and the body flew off into the air.

I once found some baby blue tits, abandoned by their mother, and kept them safe, feeding them until they could fly away. Many years later when I was at Swanky Modes (the fashion house I founded with friends), I did the same for a sparrow. I was walking home and bumped into a couple who said a baby bird had fallen out of its nest so I took it home with me and put it in a box, lined with cotton wool. I thought I might be able to work the same magic I had for the blue tits and went around the hedges, trying to find insects. Have you ever tried to do that? It's a lot harder and more time-consuming than you might think. I gave up, went to the pet shop and came back with live maggots that I hand-fed to the sparrow. It needed to be fed every couple of hours so I took it to work with me and it sat happily in the Swanky Modes studio. Over the next few weeks, it grew bigger and stronger until it started to try to fly, but I didn't feel confident about leaving it outside to be pounced on by one of the prowling neighbourhood cats. Instead I attached branches to the ceiling in my flat and tied little tins to them, filled with maggots to encourage the bird to fly and feed itself. You can imagine the amount of bird poo liberally splattered around my flat! One day, about a month after I had rescued it, I knew it was time and I opened the window and it flew away. It reminded me of the success I had with the blue tits all those years earlier.

Mum accused me of being the ringleader when we were growing up, which felt awfully unfair as my brothers seemed to escape the worst of her wrath. They were just as mischievous as I was. We were a tight unit, probably partly because of our nomadic lifestyle. We were constantly unpacking our belongings and then packing them up again, moving from my Bedford birthplace to many different counties over a 20-year period, including Lincolnshire, South Yorkshire, Warwickshire, Buckinghamshire, Kent, Huntingdonshire, Hertfordshire, Surrey and even France. Each of these houses felt like home as long as my parents and siblings were there.

We were an entrepreneurial bunch of kids. This may

have unwittingly started when Mum would pay us to tickle her feet. She promised us a penny in return for 100 tickles. I got bored very quickly but my brother Chris had his eye on the cash so he would do it along with washing up and digging the garden. He was saving up for a Scalextric set but he never got paid. I think we were mostly less motivated by money and more by entertaining ourselves but we were regularly plotting, particularly me and my sister Fiona. At Bawtry, we lived on an estate surrounded by woods with a lake and big old house at the centre, which was being used as the Officers' Mess. Our house was at the beginning of the path into the woods, which were filled with bluebells every spring. We would pick the bluebells and stand on the path, selling them to people who were off for a woodland walk. A surprising number bought them from us! We probably only charged a penny or so a bunch. At the same house we transformed the dining room into a café and charged Dad's batman (his RAF assistant) for cups of coffee, which Mum then had to reimburse him for. That was one of our less successful enterprises.

We loved an audience and would always manage to hook the interest of local children. Like the time we put a notice up charging 1d (a penny) to come into our house for a concert. That caused a small stampede amongst the neighbouring kids and they all piled in to our dining room after paying the entrance fee. The problem was we hadn't quite thought what we would do for them so we got up on the dining table and gave an improvised tap dance routine. They lapped it up but our mum was not amused. She would often encourage us though and did so when we decided to hold a Mass in the spare bedroom. We invited random children to join us and made everyone kneel down around the beds. The dressing table was the altar. We took it in turns to be the priest and the altar boy but could only remember the words '*Dominus vobiscum*' (the Lord be with you) and '*Et cum spiritu tuo*' (and with your spirit) so we just repeated that a lot until everyone got bored. I have no idea what the little kids made of it all.

It wasn't always about money. One day, we decided to set up a hospital in the dining room but we didn't have the right outfits so we borrowed Dad's big white starched handkerchiefs and fashioned them into nurses' hats. Which wouldn't have been too bad but we drew large red crosses on them using Mum's lipstick. We got in big trouble for that.

Food played a large part in our family life and home comfort. Mum was a very good cook and she had a comprehensive collection of cookbooks, including Elizabeth David, which I still have today. Elizabeth David introduced the country to a Mediterranean diet, encouraging home cooks to look beyond the tired traditional recipes compounded by years of rationing and try something new. Ingredients like basil, garlic and aubergines were bandied about, as well as the joys of olive oil, which we had to buy from a local chemist. Dad grew sweetcorn, which was impossible to get in the UK and reminded him of his childhood in South Africa.

We often helped our mum in the kitchen and as we got older, we took over occasionally – our specialty was a cracking goulash! Every Sunday we would sit down to a traditional roast and listen to the radio – the BBC comedy *Round the Horne* was a big favourite. Angus wasn't keen on meat so he would discard bits of his dinner under the table while Mum was distracted by the radio. She had a record player too and this was my introduction to pop music. I have a vivid memory of my parents going into town to buy it – a small, portable, red and cream record player – and she amassed a large, eclectic selection of records, including Ella Fitzgerald, Ray Charles, Johnny Hallyday, Anthony Perkins and Charles Aznavour, which she loved playing to us all.

I can remember the first time I tasted ketchup. We had moved to Gaydon in Warwickshire when I was five and we were in temporary accommodation while we waited for the RAF camp to finish being built. The supervisor lived on site with his wife and my dad called them squatters because they had put their caravan on land they didn't own and I had no idea what that meant then. They became good friends with us children as we roamed around happily. One unforgettable afternoon they gave us hot, salty chips with thickly buttered, sliced white bread (the first time I ate that too) and passed around a glass bottle full of blood red gloop. I helped myself to a good dollop, dipped a chip in and my taste buds went straight to heaven!

Similar taste sensations happened when we were living in France, where I tried my first sorbet. Once I ate this, I never wanted ice cream again and I am still not keen on it. We moved there when I was 11 and stayed for a couple of years, travelling back and forth from boarding school in the holidays. While there, we had an au pair who seemed very sophisticated, partly because she had an American soldier boyfriend who used to come around to visit her in a huge Chevrolet with massive fins. One day he brought with him several bottles of Coca-Cola for us. We had never tried it before and were all immediately hooked. Whether he brought it as a treat or as a bribe to get rid of us for a while, I'm not sure, but we were in love with the drink.

We were living in Fontainebleau, a town southeast of Paris and a weekend escape for frazzled city dwellers. Our first house had a tiny kitchen so my mum would put the bin outside, open the window and throw all the food waste out into it. The garden had a treehouse – which we were thrilled about – and a tortoise that we looked after and fed. We lived close to the forest of Fontainebleau, a French national park, where we went off on big walks. My brother Jeremy remembers one of us leading, out of sight, and making marks on trees and rocks to show the others where to go.

The second house we moved to was bigger, with a drive that had a large holly bush in it. An old lady used to come to the house. She would walk up the drive, stopping to cut a big bunch of holly from our bush, and then ring the doorbell, trying to sell it to us. We didn't know who she was or where she came from, but Mum called her 'Holly'. If we saw her coming, we would all hide and pretend nobody was in. Perhaps it was karma – our Bawtry bluebell sales coming back to haunt us!

Wherever we were, we all congregated at Christmas – a time for feast and celebration. There was always a big tree, a turkey in the oven and stockings from Santa Claus. One year, Dad won some money on a local raffle and bought us all big presents – Chris, Angus and I got new bikes. I can still remember the feeling of utter joy at my shiny bicycle and the excitement that my siblings had them too. What we didn't know at the time was, to save money, Dad had bought the bikes as packs that he then had to build, which made Christmas Eve incredibly stressful as he struggled to put them all together! A little while after, we had a race up the big hill outside our house. It was really steep but we all boasted that we could make it to the top. One by one my siblings fell by the wayside but I refused to give up and managed to get to the top without stopping – a bit of a metaphor for life!

CHAPTER 2

You're An Embarrassment

Memories are funny things. Often they hide in tiny, out-of-the-way places in the mind, waiting for a prompt or to catch you unawares. Sometimes they disappear completely but occasionally they can be returned by someone else, who remembers what you don't. Or who gives a different view of something that happened. While writing this book, I talked to my sister and brothers a lot about our childhood. It helped me piece together fragmented memories and understand more about how these things shaped us all. Not only how we were defined by our home life but the impact of our boarding school experiences.

Being sent away at a very young age made me emotionally detached and self-reliant – it was my coping mechanism for survival outside the family unit. This independence has been both a blessing and occasionally a curse, throughout my life but I'm not sure I would change anything even if I could. However, I know there are many boarders who have struggled with the trauma of the experience and carried it into adulthood and I can see why. I don't honestly know how I came through relatively unscathed but I think I have my family life to thank for that. It has made me extra grateful for my four siblings – the longest relationships I will have in my life. Nobody knows me better than they do.

We were all sent to boarding school, except the youngest, Jeremy. This appears to be because our parents had run out of money after educating the four older children. Both Christopher and Angus were at Ampleforth after prep school – a prestigious Catholic boarding school on the edge of the bleak North Yorkshire moors, run by Benedictine monks. Our parents had chosen the school without ever stepping inside it but Dad did once play cricket there and rather liked the pitch.

Not having had a particularly religious upbringing beforehand, the school was a bit of a shock to both boys, but it did bring the two of them closer together. To begin with they were in awe of the holiness and Chris was beguiled by the romance of the candlelit abbey, Latin text and Gregorian chant, although after a while he began to question his beliefs and whether God did indeed exist. On one occasion he went to confession to 'confess' that he didn't believe in God. The monk no doubt interpreting this as an attempt to be provocative – and not without reason, knowing Chris – told him to clear off and stop wasting his time. That was the last time that Chris ever went to confession, although that was owing to a loss of faith rather than anything that the monk said. Angus was disabused of the sanctity quite quickly after two incidents left him reeling in his first week. One of the monks was saying grace in the refectory before the boys sat down to lunch. As he was speaking, he looked out of the window and saw a cat chasing his prize ducks. Without a word, he ran out and then came back into the room with an air rifle and shot at the cat through the window. He must have caught it on the leg as it limped off and then he put the gun down and signalled for everyone to sit and eat. The second event involved an older boy, a prefect, who was outside. The same monk was walking towards him, hands tucked neatly in his cassock. As he drew level with the boy he withdrew his arm and whacked him with the heel of his hand, sending the boy staggering back and he fell, knocked out cold. He had to be taken to the infirmary.

The monks were so much stricter than the nuns at my school and my brothers reacted against the regime as they grew older – neither of them flourished there. They were always getting up to something, which usually resulted in Angus being caught but Chris often managed to evade detection and escape any blame. As a 16-year-old he would occasionally climb out of the window, fiddled the combination lock on the housemaster's bicycle and cycle down to the local village to have a pint in the pub. He had no lights and the country lanes were pitch-black. One night he veered off the road and careered down a steep bank, bending one of the pedals in the process. He got it back to the shed, refitted the lock and imagined the puzzlement of the housemaster as to how his locked bike had managed to get damaged overnight. But that was the end of his escapades to the pub.

On one notable occasion, in response to the questionable behaviour of a monk, Angus and some of the boys decided to teach him a lesson. They had been learning how to make bombs in secret and stuffed one into an empty Carnation Milk can, which they then took to the monk's greenhouse and buried in a pot. They knew his routine as he would come out every evening to check his seedlings, first switching the light on, so they wired the device to the light switch. Sure enough, that evening out he came and the boys were hidden with a good view of the greenhouse. He switched the light on and there was a terrific explosion that threw the monk backwards and rattled the little shed, blowing the panes of glass out of the windows. Thankfully the monk wasn't hurt and no one found out who was responsible.

I once went up for Exhibition Weekend (a chance for parents to visit and see their children's work) wearing a Biba minidress, which horrified Father Aiden, Chris's housemaster. He thought I would lead the boys astray as they were not used to seeing girls, let alone ones showing a lot of leg.

Anarchy definitely ruled between the three of us, but whether this was to do with our upbringing or being sent away to school, I can't honestly say. I know as I hit my teen years I was becoming a bit of a handful. As older boarders we moved back into the centre of Bedford so it felt like a sort of liberation. We would organise midnight feasts and I spent my pocket money on KitKats and Potato Puffs in the tuck shop. There were ridiculous but fun competitions too – like how many cream crackers you could eat. One of the weekly boarders had a transistor radio and we would tune in to Radio Caroline. There was general hysteria around The Beatles and everyone proclaimed their love for Paul McCartney except me – I loved John Lennon because I thought he was much cooler.

I also felt able to push boundaries like reading books that were on the banned list. I stole a book from home – *Go Tell It On The Mountain* by the American writer James Baldwin – and covered it in brown paper so the nuns couldn't tell what I was reading. Of course the sheer act of covering the book aroused suspicion and it was swiftly taken off me. I don't think I was a troublemaker or particularly difficult, but I was high-spirited. The school talked to my parents and suggested I might be happier as a weekly boarder, and have more freedom at the weekends.

As a teenager, my love of art and creating continued to grow – it really was when I was at my happiest and I could lose hours to it. I didn't think far enough ahead to consider what I was going to do with the rest of my life but I knew I wouldn't follow a conventional path. There was no pressure from my parents to focus on qualifications or aim for a respected profession. In fact, Dad regularly told me I could do or be anything I wanted to. I continued to draw and paint without interruption and became a prolific artist with many notebooks full of my work. I was focused on fashion, landscape and still life, using gouache and pencils. I also learnt how to shade.

Here's a funny story about that time and one that still amuses me to this day. It was the start of term – just before O-level exams, I think – and a girl I didn't know very well came up to me at school. She said she had something to tell me and I wondered what on earth she was about to admit to. It transpired that she had stolen some of my notebooks full of fashion drawings and had submitted them as part of her fashion application to Parsons School of Design, which was based in New York and one of the best art schools in America. She had passed my work off as her own and, incredibly, she wasn't particularly apologetic or embarrassed about what she had done. I'm not sure why she even told me as I would never have found out otherwise. I was curious to know if she had been successful. She had! So technically, I had just won a place at Parsons. Not that I would have wanted to go – I had decided I wanted to study in the UK. I wasn't cross with the girl, just flattered, but I do wonder if she ever made it to the end of the course.

Going home in the holidays held a different appeal now we were all teenagers. Everyone was physically bigger for a start and was searching for more freedom, which made it harder to return to the rules of the house and the parents' disapproving stares. There were times when it must have been like living with caged tigers who were always hungry and had too much energy. The summer holidays were blissfully long but could also be a bit dull. Christopher reminded me of a fight we had in the dining room at Brampton, where we lived when I was 15 until I left for college. He said he was bored and I told him off. I probably said something superior about only boring people being bored but he said I also told him he should use his imagination and he was incensed by this. There was a glass of sherry on the table and he picked it up and threw the contents in my face. Now it was my turn for fury and I sprang on him 'like a tiger', he remembers. Our dad heard us fighting and came in as we rolled around the floor at his feet. 'Christopher!' he said sternly. 'You shouldn't hit girls!', which rather annoyed my brother because as far as he was concerned, he was the one being hit.

Christopher did find a regular outlet for his adventurous spirit and we were in on the secret too, which was magnanimous of him. Dad had been teaching him to drive our mum's car at the local airfield. The feeling of freedom it gave him was intoxicating and he was desperate to go out on his own. One night he stole Mum's car keys and disappeared into the dark when everyone was asleep. She had a little Renault Dauphine, a sweet dodgem-style car, and Christopher would take it out on midnight jaunts around the quiet country roads. After a couple of forays, he said we could join him, so we would creep out of the front door – me, Angus and then Jeremy too when he was a bit older and we were sure we could trust him not to blab in the morning.

One night, an MG sports car overtook Christopher and he decided to race it. He went over a little bridge at the bottom of a hill, braked hard and the car span 360 degrees. Luckily, no one was hurt and no damage was done but it taught him a lesson that has stayed with him. He decided to upgrade the vehicle to our dad's sturdy Citroen Safari – a family wagon and an all-round safer beast. But it wasn't long before Dad found out his underage son with no insurance was driving his siblings around at night when they should have been in bed. I am not sure how he found out but he probably noticed the mileage had gone up. There was a bit of a scene, but Dad, quite rightly, didn't trust Christopher so he hid his car keys. This could have been the end of our midnight escapes except for one thing: as an air commodore in the RAF, my dad was assigned a driver and this particular chap was a good egg and almost part of the family. He also knew about mechanics and taught my brother how to hotwire our dad's car so he didn't need the keys. When Dad discovered Christopher's new skill, he resorted to taking something out of the engine so the car wouldn't start and then putting it back in when he wanted to use it himself. What a pain in the neck it must have been for him!

The boys were becoming increasingly unruly and Angus left the school rather suddenly. At the end of his first year of A-levels, something called a house Punch was being organised. This was an evening of entertainment put together by the boys for the other boys in the house and a few monks including the headmaster would be invited. Angus was expected to contribute and he had written a series of skits in which he planned to involve the invited monks. On the morning of the Punch, the housemaster reviewed the show and ruled out involvement of monks who were invited as part of the audience, so instead Angus went away and wrote three skits and performed them himself. In the first, he came on as a Hell's Angel, which upset a visiting Russian monk considerably. In the second, he was Hitler. In the third, he was Jesus and held his arms outstretched as if on the cross and said, 'What a way to spend Easter!' in a Liverpudlian accent before being dragged offstage. The headmaster was apoplectic and said he was going to expel Angus for blasphemy but my brother told him not to bother because he was leaving. And he did.

After his abrupt departure Angus returned to the school a year or so later for a lunch with Father Edward, his housemaster. Which was a strange turn of events as the same monk had beaten him for shoplifting when he was at school. Angus remembers bending over his chair in his pyjamas and being caned before Father Edward gave a lecture starting with 'I hope you understand why I had to do that ...' Revisiting the school brought back so many memories but it was short-lived as the headmaster got wind that Angus was on school property and phoned Father Edward to say he was not allowed on school grounds. So he was finally 'expelled' but it had had to wait for more than a year after he'd already left the school under his own steam.

⊗ ⊗ ⊗

Like many teenagers, my interest in clothes became an obsession and I began to experiment with 'looks'. As a child, my clothes were often handmade – I know how that sounds in today's world but back then it was very common. Having dresses made for you was not the bespoke luxury it is today. It was what most families did and there was always at least one person who was nifty with the sewing machine. I would also get lots of hand-me-downs from my older sister Fiona, so to have something brand new was a treat.

After a work trip to America, Dad returned with a gift for me. It was a reversible pinafore dress: on one side it was plain pink and on the other pink check. Oh, the excitement of something so foreign and sophisticated! I also remember my mum buying me two outfits from Harrods – one was a Black Watch tartan wool dress with a bow around the waist and the other was a pink jumper with a matching pink and grey check skirt. I loved them both, but I think I was more excited by the pink and grey colour combination – I have always been fixated on colour.

Mum adored clothes and followed trends. She was a big fan of Jaeger. She always looked stylish, something she was keen for me and my sister to emulate as teenagers. She introduced us to Biba, Mary Quant, Celia Birtwell and Ossie Clark, the boutique forerunners to high street fashion, and the moment I crossed their thresholds, I could see how powerful fashion was and how it encouraged self-expression through what you wore. It was the Swinging Sixties and more accessible fashion was arriving on the high street, which gave many the freedom to dress for themselves. I was influenced by these cool designers who opened their own boutiques and it planted a subconscious seed for the future.

For me, while fashion was a positive influence, what I really sought were pieces of clothing that I could adapt and transform into something unique. I did a lot of rummaging in Mum's wardrobe and would steal things from the older clothes she no longer wore in the hope that I wouldn't get found out. As soon as I started altering things she knew exactly what I was up to and put a lock on her wardrobe door. I was particularly upset at this because I had my eye on a stunning Edwardian lace dress with a high neck and little buttons down the front that I would have cut up in an instant. Instead I turned to jumble sale trawls for my weekly fashion fix. It was such a thrill to find a vintage blouse or a pair of beautifully kept 1920s shoes and it was an affordable way to dress myself. I had a strong sense of my own style and I was not afraid to use it.

Mum was horrified. She despaired of my second-hand clothing addiction and hated the outfits I created. There were so many occasions when she would refuse to walk next to me in the street because of what I was wearing.

Dad, on the other hand, did not bat an eyelid. He would give me a lift to college in his smart, chauffeur-driven car and I would skip out in all manner of outfits, including one of my charity shop favourites – a child's patchwork dressing gown worn belted as a dress, a tartan scarf and a little straw bag.

'Dressed as a peacock,' my mum would say disparagingly.

Thrift Transformations

EVERY WEEK ON *The Great British Sewing Bee* we set the contestants a transformation challenge. We give them a second-hand piece of clothing or something made of fabric that they need to work their magic on – whether it's transforming men's swimming trunks, sarongs, T-shirts, old curtains or even a parachute for the World War II themed week. It might seem easier to start with something already made and adapt it, but that's not always the case. There are many obstacles to this, whether it is the type of fabric, tailoring or seams to consider. It's one of my favourite challenges and I love seeing how everyone works within the boundaries of the piece they are given but manages to create something unrecognisable from its original state. For me, this challenge is more about imagination than it is sewing.

I have been altering clothes since I was old enough to be allowed scissors. I was driven by two things. First, I was – and still am – rather short so most garments were too long or big on me and needed adjustments. Second, I didn't want to look like everyone else so I would seek out vintage pieces to wear as they were or adapt them into something that reflected my style of the time. The truth is alteration is an incredible skill and if you find a professional who offers this, never lose their phone number! People often assume altering is easy and don't understand why it can be expensive but to do it properly is an absolute talent.

When I first started altering clothes I was really bad at it. I was impatient to transform pieces into something I could wear immediately but I didn't have the skills to do a good job – I would haphazardly cut things and bung hems up without thought or measuring. When we were young, we didn't care too much about how the clothes were finished as long as we could wear them out. There may have been an uneven hem, a chunk missing out of the back of a dress or a wonky seam but the finish wasn't important: we just wanted the outfit. It was a classic example of learning by mistake and ruining a few items along the way. Most of the time this didn't matter because I would be practising on second-hand clothes I had bought for pennies at the jumble sale, especially once Mum had locked her wardrobe. When I was about 16, I was invited to a ball and the dress code was for long gowns. I turned a crocheted blanket into a tube and made a seam at the waist to thread ribbon through to create a long skirt. My sister thought I looked very stylish and I continued to use this nifty trick for years after, particularly during the long, flowing hippy era.

It didn't take me too long to build confidence and competence so I'm glad I wasn't put off by my early attempts. And now, more than ever, as the fashion industry is under scrutiny for unsustainable practices and shocking waste, we should be saving garments from landfill by recycling and transforming them when we can. Whether you are a seasoned sewer or a complete beginner, there is such a sense of achievement in taking a redundant garment and turning it into something wearable, that could even become a favourite outfit.

Here are a few pointers from me to help you on your way:

1. **KEEP IT SIMPLE:** If you are a novice with the needle then don't start with something complicated. It's amazing how much difference changing the buttons or sewing trim onto a garment can make. You may just want to shorten a hem, embellish a lapel or cut down your jeans into shorts or skirts. Pick something easy that you can practise on and be ready to make a complete mess of it.

2. **USE YOUR IMAGINATION:** It's not just about altering something; you can create a completely different garment from the one you originally started with. Some of my favourite reinventions have been a shirt or tablecloth into a skirt and a jumper into a dress. When I was at art school I bought a kimono and turned it into a two-piece by cutting it in half. I sewed the bottom half into a skirt and made the top a jacket. The collar – made of two lengths of fabric attached at the neck and then left to hang – was remodelled by wrapping the wide strips around my waist, like a belt. At Swanky Modes, we designed an upside down cardigan so I would always recommend taking a new perspective on traditional pieces.

3. **TAKE RISKS:** The best way to discover what works is by doing it. Be prepared to take risks, make mistakes and end up with something that is not perfect but good enough. I cannot tell you how many times I have done this in the past – and how pleasantly surprised I have been when the gamble pays off.

4. **LEARN:** Alterations and adaptions are a lesson in the construction of a garment, from the pattern to the techniques used to put it together. You begin to understand the structure and this helps when you make clothes from scratch too. Once you have the knowledge then you can play around with it. Rules are there to be broken but you need to know what the rules are in the first place in order to subvert them.

5. **SOURCING:** You may have several items in your wardrobe that you are happy to sacrifice on the altar of change but if not, head for your nearest charity shop, jumble sales, car boot sales and even eBay. On your search consider the type of piece you are picking up as the cut and fabric will have a bearing on what you can do with it. Also, make sure you use the right needle and tension if you are working on something thicker like denim or anything stretchy and synthetic. All fabrics require different ways of

dealing with them but do test them with the sewing machine and the iron (some fabrics could melt, for example).

6. **PLANNING:** When considering a garment for alteration, think about what you want it to be. Draw a plan of how you envisage it and include measurements – i.e. if you are taking up the hem of a skirt, make a note of the final length you want. Try the piece on as it is, with someone else to pin, mark, etc., if possible.

7. **KIT:** You don't have to have a sewing machine but if you are tackling major alterations then it's pretty key. Whatever you do, you must get tailor's chalk to mark out on fabric, pins, needles, different coloured threads, a tape measure and scissors.

8. **NEW TECHNIQUES:** If there is something you want to try but are not sure how to do it, don't discount it. Take a look at the brilliant reference books available for sewers and check out YouTube for great tutorials. Don't forget programmes like *The Great British Sewing Bee* too!

9. **EASY WINS:** I'm a big fan of mending. Now more than ever we should be making our clothes last and not ditching them at the first sign of a hole. Invisible

mending is incredibly difficult to do so make a feature of it instead and this can become an art in itself. I would much rather embrace the imperfection and use a different thread or a vibrant patchwork to draw attention to the difference. Clothes moths seem impossible to get rid of these days and my jumpers have become a victim so I often darn them with a clashing embroidery thread, which is incredibly satisfying. Felting is another technique I use, either with knitting wool, embroidery wool thread or a special felting wool, which does require tools but works brilliantly.

10. **PRACTISE WITH A FRIEND:** You will help and learn from each other, grow in confidence and inspire each other to try new things. Collaboration is something I have benefited from throughout my career and it can help you too.

11. **HAVE FUN:** Enjoy the process – and be brave!

CHAPTER 3
London Calling

I left the convent school after my O-levels. I can't remember what my results were, which is funny because I didn't get many of them so it shouldn't be too difficult. I wasn't good at exams and I struggled with several key subjects, particularly languages, including Latin, which was my worst. Perhaps this was connected to my deafness because the rest of my family are so good at them – I'm the only one who is hopeless. When Angus and I went travelling around Europe (of which, more later in this chapter), he would be able to pick up words and phrases quickly and managed entire conversations in Italian without ever having learnt it. This is a skill I don't possess.

It has always been about creativity for me. There was never any doubt in my mind that it was where my future lay. I had no idea about the fashion industry or possible career paths or whether I was even good enough, I just knew there was nothing else I wanted to do. I had my heart set on art school but I needed to do a foundation course to get in, plus my exam results were too low so I had to do an A-level to boost my scores. If I could pass the A-level and amass a great portfolio then these things combined should be enough to get me through the doors of one of the most respected art schools of the time – not that I knew who they were.

Cambridge Art College was the nearest place to where my parents were living then. I was still only 16 so it made sense to stay at home while studying and those two years were the longest I had spent with my parents since I was five. It was such a happy experience, maybe because I hadn't lived at home for so long, and I got to spend time with Jeremy too, who was excited to have me around. And they were not strict, oppressive parents either. They were pleased to have me back and very relaxed about where I was, so I could come and go as I pleased, sometimes staying with friends in Cambridge.

When I was at home, my dad would often make me breakfast, usually a plate of perfectly scrambled eggs. And Mum would enlist my sewing skills – I used to handmake her Christmas present every year until one year I didn't have time and gave her a glass vase instead: 'At last, a real present!' she said.

One of the most notable outfits I made for her was when I was 16 and my parents were invited to a big fancy dress party. We settled on a Super Hero look so I made her hot pants, a hooded cape and created false boots – like long spats – to go over her shoes, attached under the sole by a strip of elastic like a stirrup. I have a photo of her as the gorgeous caped crusader, dancing exuberantly at the party, full of joy. Mum was a tricky woman but it's good to be reminded of how much fun she was too. She was a great host and they often had friends over for cocktails before they all went out for dinner. Once they had left, us older siblings would go around finishing the dregs. I haven't been able to drink whisky since, it put me right off!

Art college was a revelation. Suddenly I was drawing and making things all day, every day. There were no interruptions for boring lessons I had no interest in, although I still had to pass my A-level, which meant the pressure of an exam looming at the end of the two years. I immersed myself in all the different mediums on offer, including fine art, printing and lots of work with colour. We had a fabulous life drawing teacher who made us look at things differently, like studying the space around the figure as well as the body itself. The college had a great reputation for graphics and illustration too so there was a slight bias towards this area and I slid into it. The place attracted world-renowned tutors and turned out a great number of excellent illustrators, including two lads who would go on to create the iconic *Spitting Image* – Roger Law and Peter Fluck. I became great mates with Candy Amsden, who was on my foundation course. Candy's sister Deirdre is a British art quiltmaker who forged links with the Soweto Sisters, an African makers' collective, and was married to Roger Law. When I set up Swanky Modes a few years later, Candy was teaching art at Holloway Prison and we have kept in touch over the years.

The college organised lots of bus trips to museums and galleries – places that filled me with inspiration and the desire to create better work. I also regularly visited the Museum of Archaeology and Anthropology in Cambridge, an absolute favourite of mine. There was over 2 million years of human history behind glass and I loved the combination of other cultures and ancient artefacts. I could lose myself for hours wandering around and sketching as I went, unaware of what was going on around me. On one occasion a group of men arrived, looking rather out of place, not the usual student visitors. I was trying to get around them to leave the building but they were making a bit of a fuss and stopped me walking past. In their midst was a very recognisable figure – Prince Charles had come into the museum. He saw my surprise and said to his security, 'It's fine, let her go.' How frustrating for him to be ushered around everywhere, I thought as I left, free as a bird.

A career in fashion had still not occurred to me at this point but clothes were an important part of my life. A jumble sales regular, I picked up the most fantastic bargains, many of them fab vintage pieces. My eye was on anything I could wear as it was or cut up and alter so I made lots of mini-skirts and shortened fitted coats. I would scour the stalls for pre-war dresses, especially gems from the 1930s. When I think about what the original pieces would be worth now, I shudder, but then they were being thrown out and we didn't see them as antiques of the future. It was recycling and to me it felt sensible to give them a new life and reinterpret them in my style. My sister Fiona can remember our mum being horrified once when she came to meet me for lunch and I was wearing a tablecloth! A beautifully embroidered vintage piece, I had turned it into a long skirt and threaded ribbon around the top to create a waistband.

I started partying when I went to art college in 1965 and I didn't really slow down until the mid-1980s. If there was live music, I would be there with a few glasses of cheap barley wine – a very strong beer – or shots of neat Martini. I was totally open to all sorts of music – I loved bands like Fleetwood Mac, Chris Farlowe and The Animals – and if it was at an outdoor venue, even better. On one painful occasion, I trekked to Woburn Abbey in Hertfordshire with my then boyfriend for the infamous music festival, one of the original 'hippy' gatherings that drew incredible headline acts. The weekly music magazine, *Melody Maker*, had listed Jimi Hendrix as the Saturday night name and Fleetwood Mac were performing on Sunday. Can you believe we turned up without tickets? I'm not sure what we were thinking, whether we thought we could buy them on the door or would be able to bunk over the fence, I don't know. What I do remember is the crashing disappointment when we were turned away. Jimi was there somewhere, tuning his guitar and limbering up for his big stage moment and we wouldn't get to see him. Sadly, he died a couple of years later so there's a lingering regret. At least we didn't miss Fleetwood Mac as they cancelled at the last minute, blaming a clash of schedules – anyway, I had seen them previously.

There is often a close connection between music and art, one breeding the other or entwined in some way. This was evident at Cambridge Art College, particularly for one of its students, Syd Barrett, and his pal David Gilmour, who was studying English at the technical college. They would spend lunchtimes writing music and jamming on their guitars. When they left, the year I joined, they formed their band Pink Floyd and hit the underground music scene with growing success. I had friends who knew Syd and they brought his record, 'Arnold Layne', in before it was released, so when the news broke that they were returning to college for the Christmas party, I bought a ticket, which cost about 38p. The event was called The Art School Psychedelic Freak Out and the ex-students returned as Pink Floyd and set up in the life drawing studio, which was big enough to take an audience and had a stage. The psychedelic light show was created by using coloured oils that swirled around, reacting to the heat from the projector and the perfect backdrop for several numbers including. It was a tight, hot, sweaty squeeze in that room and the music vibrated through us – it was so loud and I loved it!

I played hard, but I worked hard too. By now we were at the tail end of the sixties and I was thinking about art schools. My college suggested I apply to St Martin's (as they were known then before they merged with Central in 1989) based on their fantastic reputation and good Graphics department, a direction they were gently pushing me into. I hadn't done any research on where to go and the courses that were available but London called to me – the thought of being in the midst of it, studying, hanging out, late-night clubs and gigs every night. I sent my portfolio to St Martin's and was then called for an interview to the 1930s purpose-built school on Charing Cross Road. The more I saw of the school, the more I wanted to go there. I was accepted on the three-year Graphics and Illustration course and a whole new world opened up to me.

Around this time my parents moved to Warlingham in Surrey and I moved with them initially. Dad was working for the Ministry of Defence and was driven into London every day so it was easy for me to hitch a ride with him and it meant we had time to chat. He was pleased that I was following my dream, maybe because his had almost been scuppered by his own dad, and he could see how happy I was. After a few months I realised how hard it was to maintain a London art school social life and still catch the last train back to Surrey so I moved in with a friend in Muswell Hill. My dad paid my rent, which was about £4 a week. We lived at the top of her parents' house – a little attic flat – and had complete freedom, which we took full advantage of. Through her, I met Harry Maslin who, at that time, was a sound engineer in Philadelphia before moving to New York to be a music producer.

He worked with all the greats, including David Bowie, Dionne Warwick, Carly Simon and Barry Manilow, and would come to London to hear UK talent, such as The Who. I met him in London and then flew to New York to visit him at his studio before staying with him at his home in Philadelphia – we were good friends. We once went to the cinema, via the pet shop, because he needed to pick up supper for his pet snake. He bought a live mouse and then we went to see *2001: A Space Odyssey*. At the end we realised the mouse had eaten its way out of the box and escaped. I hope it lived a long and happy life, watching movies and snacking on popcorn crumbs!

St Martin's was everything I had hoped it would be and so much more. It was the most amazing community of students and teachers, who were bursting with creativity, life force and a healthy streak of rebellion. The café at the heart of the school was where everyone mixed and cross fertilisation between the Painting, Graphics, Sculpture, Fashion and Foundation courses was encouraged. There were weekly events and socials too, like the Friday night film club at St Martin's, which showed French black-and-white and surrealist films followed by rigorous discussions about them.

My Graphics degree incorporated many different areas, including Film, Animation, Design, Typography and Illustration – all subjects that have their own dedicated courses now. I learnt so many different techniques and skills that I still call on today. I didn't waste a moment and can honestly say I enjoyed every lesson, but I was particularly fascinated by animation and photography. My photography teacher, Dermot Goulding, was amazing, as was his assistant, who I modelled for – my first experience of fashion in front of the camera. One year I designed the St Martin's Christmas party invitation, using my typography skills, which was a bit of an honour but also a bigger bit of pressure! There was an annual Christmas pantomime that required students and staff to act together. One year a giant cake was wheeled on at the end and one of the students, a girl with big breasts, jumped out of it stark-naked. I have never forgotten that and I'm quite sure most of the audience haven't either. I suppose that wouldn't happen now, but back then we just regarded it as fun, as long as no one was forced to do something they didn't want to.

⊗ ⊗ ⊗

We were on the cusp of the 1970s and, after the swinging, sexy sixties, our generation were trailblazing into the new decade in a streak of sequins and safety pins. Soho was at the heart of it all. By day I would pop into the French shop on Old Compton Street, which sold the rarest of cheeses at that time – Brie. It was hard to get hold of, so I would buy a wedge to take back to my mum whenever I went home. I also went to Berwick Street Market to the old haberdashery stall to pick up beads, ribbons, brocade and small pieces of embroidery. The stallholders knew we were students from St Martin's because of the way we dressed and this is still true today. But it wasn't just clothes I experimented with, I gave myself regular haircuts too. During college my hair was long, almost to my waist, with my signature fringe, but when I went to art school, I plucked my eyebrows completely out and styled the centre strip of my hair into a Mohican. My hair was still long but I got rid of the parting and fringe and had a strip of hair that stood up spikily – I was punk before Punk!

Soho at night was a different, pulsating, vibrant story. I embraced the club, bar and live music scenes and particularly loved mixing in liberating gay, trans and party circles. We would frequent all the places with big reputations like The Colony Room, the Coach and Horses and The French House – known locally as 'The Triangle', the only three drinking holes you needed.

The Colony Room was affectionately nicknamed Muriel's after the infamous nightclub owner Muriel Belcher, who ran it. It was halfway up Dean Street, one of the arteries of roads off Old Compton Street, and you would almost miss the ordinary front door that opened onto a steep, narrow staircase leading to the dingy, tiny first-floor bar. The walls were painted an unattractive green and the atmosphere of 'anything goes and often did' was intoxicating. There behind the bar was Muriel; loud, camp and usually very rude. She filled the private members' club with friends, like Francis Bacon – who immortalised her in several of his paintings, Alan Bennett and Jonathan Miller. My boyfriend's music teacher used to play piano there so we went occasionally and were in awe of it.

My other favourite haunt was The French House, known as 'The French'. This was at the bottom end of Dean Street and is still an integral, beloved part of the Soho scene today. Since 1989 it has been run by Lesley Lewis, a long-time Soho resident and matriarch of the community. I met Lesley many years ago and asked her to model for Swanky Modes. She used to have a cabaret act with snakes – one of them was a python – before running a strip joint called the Carnival Club. I still pop in to see her, she pours me a glass of prosecco on the house and we catch up on all the Soho gossip.

In my late twenties I gave up drinking for five years. I didn't have a serious problem but I knew it was a little out of hand so I took a break. I returned to the Coach and Horses one evening with a boyfriend and decided to order something alcoholic – but what exactly after all those teetotal years? Someone suggested Advocaat, thinking the creaminess of the eggs and sugar would make it taste more like I was drinking custard and not hard alcohol. I went up to the bar and ordered it and the barman said, 'If you ever come in here and order that drink again, I won't serve you.'

It was good to be back in 'The Triangle'!

My first long-term boyfriend was Colin, who was on my Graphics course. He was blonde, good-looking and, most importantly, a lot of fun. His inherent sense of style verged on flamboyance, which was everyday normal at St Martin's but not ideal walking through the rougher east London streets of his home. He would wear an enormous coat over his outfit, even when the weather didn't require it, and then emerge from it, butterfly-like, when he got to school. I was a big fan of Colin. We were a couple while we were studying but we weren't in each other's pockets, we just liked hanging out together. He was a very talented artist, wrote songs and had an amazing voice – all things I found incredibly attractive – and we shared a passion for live music, going to as many gigs as we could afford. I would go back to the East End with him to visit his family and sit in their local boozer, where his grandmother played the piano.

Colin turned out to be gay. I know this may sound unlikely but I had no idea and I'm not sure he did either to begin with. Or maybe he did and was hiding it because of the prejudice against gay people and the pressure many were under to be heterosexual. This is still an issue today. Luckily the circles we moved in then were much more open-minded. I had managed to convince my GP to prescribe me the contraceptive pill, which was notoriously hard to get at that time, but I must have been pretty persuasive. It was totally liberating. Colin and I broke up after we left St Martin's but we remained the best of friends and he helped in the early days of Swanky Modes. He did some illustrating for us, sang in the backing band for our fashion shows and continued to be the best company. Sadly, he died several years ago and I still miss him.

Even as poor students we managed to go away on holiday. I'm ashamed to tell this story but in the interests of truth and by way of a belated (50 years) apology to my brother (who reminded me of this recently), I shall. Colin and I decided to go to France but I was absolutely skint so I borrowed a significant sum from 18-year-old Christopher. He had earned it by washing up in Warlingham Park, a psychiatric hospital, and continued to work there while I swanned off on holiday with his money. Once I was back, he would occasionally, politely, remind me that I owed him some money, to which I would ask him to stop hassling me. He thinks my conscience got the better of me about 15 years later and I repaid him, with an adjustment for the substantial inflation there had been in the 1970s – even now I'm a little mortified.

I think this was the same French holiday when we decided to hitchhike to Barcelona. We were about halfway down France and were picked up by a guy who seemed fine. After a while he asked if we would mind him making a pit stop as he had to do some business. He gave us some cakes to eat while we waited and we ate them. Big mistake. I threw up out of the car window but Colin was almost unconscious and I was scared. The driver of the car had returned at this point and I said my boyfriend was really poorly so he said he knew just where to take him. I didn't know whether to trust him or not but thank goodness

I didn't. Instead I followed them and made a big scene, shouting at the driver, who let Colin go and we ran for it. We went straight to the local police station to report the incident and they just laughed at us.

This experience didn't put me off travelling. Or hitchhiking. At any opportunity I would do both. I couldn't afford conventional travel so I would hitchhike regularly, either on my own or with someone else. It was just what we did, not really a big deal and very relaxed in those days. I know it's different now.

In the summer of 1970 I went travelling with Angus and my then boyfriend Phil. Oh, and a journalist who lived in our squat who was driving to Istanbul (and who was tragically murdered in America a few years later during an undercover investigation). Our plan was to get to Malta so he took us as far as Dubrovnik and then we got a boat to Italy and hopped out at the port of Bari. As we were heading away from the harbour, a group of sailors walked past us and one of them grabbed my breasts. I was in shock: what just happened there?

We hitchhiked to the south of Italy and caught a boat to Malta. We had to hand our passports over to the captain, which seemed a little unusual but we didn't question it. We were planning to head to Gozo to meet a college pal of mine and Angus got chatting to a guy in a brass band, who offered us a lift. Not wanting to miss the opportunity, when we docked, we raced off the boat to keep up with him. We assumed we would be reunited with our passports at border control but we were sent back to the boat to retrieve them. When we got there the captain and crew were furious, accusing us of jumping ship and refused to return our passports. At this juncture we could have, and probably should have, bribed them but we didn't have enough money and I don't know if that would have worked. Instead we stayed on the boat overnight with a member of the crew guarding us, before they sailed back to Italy in the morning with us on board. We then hitchhiked back through Italy to Switzerland before catching a train to the UK.

We never did get to Malta.

The trip that remains seared in my memory was the time I went to the USA. I was at St Martin's and had met an American girl, who invited me to go and stay with her in Washington, D.C. I jumped at the chance and spent some time with her and her Afro-Caribbean boyfriend. Through them, I met their friends, Perry, an African-American, and Bill and we would all go out to clubs together.

Being with them introduced me to a level of racism I had obviously not witnessed as a middle-class white woman. In one bar the barman was incredibly rude to my friend's boyfriend and refused to serve him because he was black. He dealt with this sort of abuse on a daily basis but that evening he snapped and disappeared to the loo. Something happened to the electrics and the building appeared to lose power at the same time he came back and told us to grab our stuff and make a run for it.

I had a great time and really enjoyed hanging out with Bill and Perry too – Perry had broken his leg in a motorbike accident so was hobbling around on crutches. They were being paid to drive a car to Mexico City to deliver it to its owner and asked if I wanted to join the road trip. I thought it would be a blast and it was, sort of. The levels of racism aimed at Perry continued, and if anything got worse, it was unbelievably shocking. On the journey we stopped off at a bar and the barman told me we must sit separately. He was being kind, explaining that otherwise Perry would get picked on for being with white people and Bill and I would get abuse for mixing with someone of colour. What no one realised was that Bill was also of mixed heritage and had an important job, teaching African-Americans how to get into college. This set the tone for the rest of the trip. Wherever we were it was the same thing – for example, when we stopped to change a tyre I had to hide behind the car so he didn't get shouted at.

There were lovely moments on the road trip too and a fantastic overnight stay with a family in New Orleans who were so welcoming. The woman gave me plastic necklaces that were given out from the floats during Mardi Gras – I have still got those necklaces after all this time. There was one incident in a bar there where the barman took one look at Perry and said they didn't serve 'people on crutches'.

I didn't expect us to have race issues in New Orleans.

By the time we reached the Mexican border we

were pretty wise to the general racism and corruption surrounding us so it was no surprise that they were prepared to let me through but not Perry. Until we returned with $20 tucked into my passport and this time they let us all through. We flew back from Mexico to Washington but had to change planes at Texas, which meant going through border control. It was the first and, to date, only time I was strip-searched – it was assumed the company I was keeping must make me a drugs mule.

I took this trip a year or so after Martin Luther King Jnr. was assassinated but nothing much seemed to have changed.

CHAPTER 4

Squats and Motorbikes

The seventies arrived in a fanfare of expectation and excitement after the liberating sixties but this was swiftly followed by a growing feeling of unrest and disillusionment across the country. Rising living costs were matched by climbing unemployment numbers and there was a severe housing crisis which resulted in limited affordable rental options. This pushed some to make temporary homes in unoccupied buildings. During this time it was estimated over 30,000 people in London[1] were living in squats and I was one of them.

It's now referred to as the Golden Age of Squatting but back then it was just what we did and we all had our own reasons – me, my friends, my brothers, people working in creative industries, low income families, the homeless. It wasn't illegal. Up until 2012 it was a civil issue until a change of law made squatting a criminal offence. Before then the only crime was breaking and entering but if you gained access without damage and then changed the locks that didn't count, in fact it gave you certain rights as

---

1   History Workshop Journal: Sisterhood and Squatting in the 1970s.

a key holder. It was rare that a privately owned property was targeted. Many of the squats were in council-owned properties and in some instances squatters were encouraged to become part of a housing co-operation, which meant the local authorities would give them a payment to keep the place habitable. In many ways it was the perfect arrangement.

The Family Squatting Campaign, launched in 1968, was a godsend for homeless families waiting on the council house list and it became a precursor to the housing association. Single parents, mainly women, could join forces to create a happy 'commune', where they would help each other with childcare, cooking and emotional support. There was a strong feminist network that grew over this time too. For me, it wasn't a political statement (although we railed against the Tory government and greedy, unscrupulous landlords), a parental rebellion or my only option, it was a cheap, practical solution to living and working in London.

It was popular amongst those of us in creative industries – artists, musicians, writers, actors – which meant accidental communities of like-minded people would pop up all over the city, but there were also people who had office jobs, worked in the emergency services or in accounting, for example. It was a vibrant and refreshing way to live but it came with a dark underbelly that I was constantly aware of: embracing all aspects of society, including the more dangerous combination of the militant disaffected, drug dealers and addicts. I would steer well clear of any toxic presence. There was a mutual respect amongst squatters, a tacit understanding, and I rarely felt uncomfortable or unsafe. My brothers saw a slightly different side but I was never burgled, attacked or threatened throughout my entire squatting 'career'.

My brother Angus was the first of us to live in a squat. Just 18, he was at home for Christmas after leaving Ampleforth boarding school in disgrace, when he slipped out of the house one snowy night and disappeared. When my parents woke up and discovered he was missing they went outside and there, in the snow, he had written 'ANGUS' before he escaped. He rang me to say he had left home and I told him to get in touch with our parents, who were beside themselves with worry. He did call them but refused to finish his education or return home. Rather strangely, as he put the phone down, my mum got a crossed line and could hear an Irishman talking so she was convinced Angus had been taken by the IRA, possibly as some long-held retribution towards her dad. She was beside herself and had no idea how to track Angus down so she told a friend who was a black cab driver and he alerted the rest of the cabbies so everyone kept an eye out. In fact, resourceful Angus had already found a room to rent and a job before he absconded.

Angus was paying £2-a-week rent for a room in a house with a shared bathroom and kitchen and a broken window in his bedroom so when his mate Simon, a fireman, suggested moving into a squat together, he figured it couldn't be worse than where he already was and, more importantly, it was a rent-free opportunity to live with friends.

Simon had found a great place on Elgin Avenue, W9 – number 13, which was part of a terrace of empty Greater London Council-owned properties. The houses were tall, early Victorian piles, with basements and attics which had been left empty for years. Angus met Simon and a few others at the house and they knew they had to secure it there and then before more people came with the same idea and moved in. They needed a volunteer to stay overnight and protect the house while the others got their stuff and Angus offered. It was winter and there was no heating but someone had brought a two-bar electric fire so he settled down in front of it in his sleeping bag. In the middle of the night he rolled over onto it and woke to find his sleeping bag was on fire. Mistakenly thinking it was somebody else who was set alight, he shouted, 'Wake up, you fool, you're on fire!' before realising it was him and managing to douse the flames. He then got back into his wet sleeping bag, which now had a large charcoaled hole at the bottom of it, and went back to sleep.

There was someone already in the house when Angus and his pals moved in. A homeless man was living in squalor in the basement and it was pretty grim. An ex-boxer whose humanity had all but been stripped from him, he would spend his days roaming the streets mugging women – there was a pile of discarded handbags in the fireplace. Angus wasn't sure what to do with him but he had heard of an attic space available a couple of doors down so he cleaned it up, painted the walls and put new locks on the bedroom door. The homeless man was happy to move into it but didn't stay long before he disappeared.

Angus definitely experienced the seedier side of squat living. Twice he was there when the front door was kicked in: once by a couple of men with guns who may have been undercover police on the search for an Irishman who had left the house a week before; and then a man and his son looking for an axe-wielding thug who had attacked his daughter but who definitely wasn't hiding in the house.

Angus was also burgled twice but figured this might have happened wherever he lived so it didn't put him off. He did take in the occasional homeless person and offer them a room for a few nights until the time he caught one of the guys rummaging in his friend's handbag. He asked him what he was doing and the man said he was looking for matches. Angus knew this was a lie and the man knew he knew too so he picked up a chair and swung it at Angus. He never invited waifs and strays to stay after that.

Angus was still so young. He was working on Oxford Street during the day selling suits, and at Dingwalls music club in Camden as a barman at night. The schedule took its toll and before too long, the shop boss wanted to know what was going on and did his mother know what he was up to, so he left and focused on club work. One night he rode his motorbike through the door of Dingwalls (reminiscent of our dad riding a horse into the hospital, many years earlier), into the bar and onto the dance floor amongst the guests. He ran straight into the owner, Tony Mackintosh, who demanded he put his bike away and come to his office immediately. Convinced he was about to get the sack, Angus stood in front of Tony, who told him, 'That was fantastic! When word gets out, people are going to flock here but don't ever pull a stunt like that again.'

He kept his job.

At the age of 25, I left my parents' house in Surrey and moved into number 13 to join Angus. My boyfriend, Phil, came too. My burgeoning fashion business was taking every penny I had so this seemed like a sensible solution. The three of us shared the ground floor and basement, with a kitchen. The floors above us had their own kitchen too and so we were fairly self-contained. We would cook and eat together sometimes and there was a gas meter we kept fed with coins – it was all very civilised. Phil and I had a tiny room so we built our bed on scaffolding poles we had found in the garden and put a rail in underneath for clothes and set up a desk.

Simon and his girlfriend still lived there and we spent time with them. And Martin and Sue lived on the middle floor. Martin was in the illegal exotic animal trade and kept ferrets, snakes and even baby crocodiles in the bathtub. If you went into their room you needed your wits about you – and string to tie around your trouser legs in case something went up them! Angus was once confronted by a black-and-white snake as it slithered down the staircase and towards the front door. Months later, he found it in the front garden, hibernating under a piece of corrugated iron.

All of the houses in the terrace were squats and full of the most eclectic mix of people. At number 3 the artist and campaigner Caroline Coon, who even inspired songs to be written about her, set up Release, an agency offering legal support for youths charged with drug possession. I remember a protest on the roof involving anti-vaccines campaigner Piers Corbyn that was focused on the eviction of Elgin Avenue tenants. Joe lived at number 5. He sold eggs out of the back of his Morris Minor van. He had been a roadie for a band but was disillusioned by how hard the music industry was and he didn't think the group he was working for – Queen – had a future.

My brother Christopher moved into number 5. He has since said that he wouldn't have had the nerve to do it if we hadn't led the way and he was reassured by having Angus and I close by. He had been offered a management consultancy job in the City but wasn't due to start for a few months and needed a job in the interim. As he had a maths degree, he applied to be a supply maths teacher at Holland Park School – renowned as it was the same school Labour politician Tony Benn's children went to and his wife, Caroline, was chair of the board of governors. He arrived in the middle of a week, in the middle of a term, and on that first day he was given a bunch of keys to his classroom, a pile of textbooks and was left to get on with it. He had no training or experience and had to ask one of the other teachers which of the textbooks he should use for his first lesson of the day. Having been hired as a 'supply' teacher, he had only expected to fill in for the random absences of other teachers, but such was the shortage of maths teachers at that time that he was drafted in to undertake a proper teaching role, as if he were fully trained. This required some fast on-the-job learning for him and he coped, but it really was far from ideal that the school had to resort to employing someone so lacking in relevant experience.

Our parents came to visit us in our squat homes. I'm not sure what they expected. It felt like a royal visit as Dad walked around, wearing his tweed jacket and smart twill trousers, hands behind his back. He took it all in quietly until he stepped in a pile of cat sick, at which point he exclaimed, 'Oh CHRIST!' – it was the only thing he said the entire time. Mum blamed the sixties; she thought our heads had been turned by the freedom of it all. She may have had a point because neither our elder sister nor younger brother were tempted to squat, unlike the three of us. Unimpressed as my parents were by our living conditions, they didn't try to talk us out of it. Maybe the fact that the three of us were together was enough to stop them worrying, or perhaps they just washed their hands of the whole sorry business.

Chris started his respectable job in the City but he was

still a maverick and approached everything with his own brand of individuality. He would head off to work on a motorbike in a pair of golden and sparkling Biba wellies and a leather jacket and change when he got to the office. The U bend had broken off the back of his toilet one day, making it unusable, so he'd become a regular, so to speak, at the public loo nearby, which very inconveniently closed at night, at which time it became a public inconvenience, as far as Chris was concerned. It was a vaguely amusing aspect of squat living at the time and a pal of his mentioned it to a friend who was also a producer for BBC TV *Arena*, a new documentary series. They were keen to do something on squats and came over for a chat, but while the original idea came to nothing, they asked to do something with me instead, which there will be more of later.

The Greater London Council (GLC), who owned the properties we were squatting in, did attempt to get us evicted from number 13 and so we went to the High Court to meet a judge and discuss our case. At the first hearing we won but the next time, a year later, we weren't so lucky and were served an eviction notice.

Angus moved into number 5, where Chris lived. They had a close brotherly relationship by this time so it was a complete surprise to Chris when he bumped into a neighbour who broke the news that Angus was getting married the following day. It was the first Chris had heard of it and he assumed it was a joke – it wasn't. Angus confirmed his wedding was booked and asked Chris to be a witness. Straight after the registry office, Angus suggested they all go to the pub, but the bride had better things to do and didn't join them. The wedding was the one and only time that Chris ever met the bride, whose name was Brandy Gardes.

Brandy was an American roadie who worked for Marc Bolan, lead singer of T. Rex who died, aged 29, on 16 September 1977 when a car driven by his girlfriend, singer Gloria Jones, hit a tree in south-west London. Brandy's visa was about to run out so she figured the best way to solve the issue was to marry a British man. She asked Angus as she said she preferred to marry someone she knew rather than a complete stranger and after a short deliberation, he agreed. Marc Bolan died soon after and Brandy returned to the States. Many years later, Angus was looking at a book about American truckers – *Big Rigs* – and there was Brandy Young, his first wife. She had built an amazing truck business! It's funny how things turn out.

My brothers were on the fringes of some musical circles and some of the musicians were starting bands which went on to become quite well known, such as The Clash and The Sex Pistols. Chris first met Sex Pistols bassist Sid Vicious when Mick Jones of The Clash brought him round for a cuppa at Chris' squat. Chris walked in, saw Sid sitting on the sofa and asked if he was a refugee from the Hare Krishna Temple – with his shaved head, he looked like one of their devotees. Mick was alarmed and took Chris aside, warning him that you don't say things like that to Sid because it might turn nasty. A few months later, towards the end of 1976, Chris thought that the writing was on the wall and that the Elgin Avenue properties were about to be taken back by the GLC. He knew Sid was keen to move from the small Shepherds Bush squat where he was living, to the grander proportions and better location of Elgin Avenue, even if it would only be for a short time. So they swapped squats. Unfortunately for Chris, the gamble didn't pay off: he came home to Shepherds Bush one night to find his belongings on the pavement and new locks on the door while Sid lived blissfully on at number 5 Elgin Avenue. Maybe 'blissfully' is not exactly an appropriate word to describe Sid's state of mind. Within a couple of years he would die from a drugs overdose in New York, while out on bail, having been charged with murdering his girlfriend Nancy Spungen.

There were a couple of robberies in the house after Sid moved in and everyone thought it may have been him. One day, Angus, discovering his record collection had disappeared, went to Sid's room to ask what was going on. The room was empty, but there were some guitars lying around, so he picked one up and sold it as compensation for his records. Sid wasn't too happy, especially as he claimed the guitar was a highly sought-after Les Paul, and accused Angus of taking it, which was quite scary, but nothing happened in the end.

I lived in squats for several years, mainly in west, north-west and north London, and they fell into three categories

– the good, the bad and the ugly. One of the best was a beautiful but shabby Edwardian House in Brondesbury, north Kilburn, which had a summer house in the garden that had come from the Great Exhibition of London in 1851 – I never wanted to leave there. I look back on this time with such fondness. We were lucky – I didn't realise quite how lucky we were – but when I compare it to now, it's so much more difficult to settle in a city. Back then, friends of mine were buying houses in London and Chris got a mortgage from the GLC, benefiting from a Labour government. A few years later, Angus benefited from the Tory rule when he bought an ex-council house. It wasn't out of reach for people with ordinary jobs or freelancers in the creative world to get on the housing ladder. Now it is a very different story.

During our squat years we all had motorbikes, sometimes there was one half-built in the kitchen or a couple taken apart in the front garden. I have never learnt how to drive a car. Maybe it's because I have lived in London all my adult life and am spoilt by the public transport system but it's not something I have ever felt I needed to do. Or maybe it's because I rode motorbikes instead. There's a particular thrill from two wheels that you don't get from four.

I got into bikes because of Phil. After I graduated from St Martin's, I was living back at home and was in the process of setting up a new business, Swanky Modes. Phil lived up the road from me and I met him in the local pub. A motorbike mechanic who bought, did up and sold bikes and then raced them in his spare time, he would come and pick me up on one of his bikes and we would speed through Surrey in search of adventure. Okay, I know usually you wouldn't put the words 'Surrey' and 'adventure' together in the same sentence! Anyway, one hot summer day, I was sunbathing in just my knickers in Phil's garden when he persuaded me to come out for a bike ride. It was a glorious day and we were impatient to get on the road so I didn't bother to find my shoes, or even clothes for that matter. Instead I wrapped a scarf around my breasts as a makeshift top and hopped on the back of his bike. Several minutes later, somewhere in the middle of Surrey, the scarf slipped to my waist and we continued with me accidentally topless and wearing just my pants.

Who says you can't find adventure in the Home Counties?

I learnt to ride a motorbike on a BSA Bantam when I was 21. I was lucky to pass because when I took my test, I did a wheelie going up the hill but the driving examiner didn't see me or it would have been an instant fail. That said, I was a great biker! I owned various motorbikes over the years, like a Yamaha and an Italian bike that wasn't a Ducati, much to my disappointment. My social life with Phil became very motorbike focused too. We would take regular trips away, touring around and staying in army tents. During the Queen's Silver Jubilee celebration of 1977 we were in Wales and saw the beacons lit, looking beautiful along the rugged coast. We went to a Dublin road race and also, for several years, to the Isle of Man TT race (and the amateur version). Once we had an impromptu race between our group of friends. I was the only woman, and had the smallest bike, so they unanimously agreed I should have a head start in the race. They gave me ten minutes and everyone following had staggered starts depending on the size of their bike. They didn't overtake me so they assumed I had pulled over somewhere and taken myself out of the race. Maybe it had all been too much for me. Instead, when they got to the finish, I was already there. I had won! I was incredibly pleased with myself but one of the group was absolutely furious and shouted about an unfair advantage.

My old art college pal Candy Amsden and her boyfriend Alf were part of our motorbike gang. We called ourselves Club Degenerate and I made T-shirts for us. I screen printed black tyre tracks onto white T-shirts and painted the capitals DG in red, finishing with a good spattering of red paint. Little did I know when I made them at Swanky Modes that they would inspire my then assistant Steven Noble, who worked for us before going on to become a costume designer in film. When he was working on the movie *Bridget Jones's Baby* (2016), he was organising the costume for the women's rights march scene and remembered my T-shirts. He had a version of them made up and dressed the protesters in them!

When I moved to London in 1974, I took my motorbike

and Phil with me. I would ride around town, buzzing through the traffic on Swanky Modes errands during the day and going off to gigs in the evening. I found the perfect evening outfit for motorbike travel: a leopard-skin catsuit! Nothing says 'party' like an all-in-one animal print and it was so comfortable for pillion riding and dancing.

I only fell off my motorbike once. It was in Notting Hill and I had overtaken a bus. I looked back for a split second and saw the bus driver – he was incredibly handsome – so this distracted me for a second more. I crashed into the car in front, came straight off my bike and ended up sprawled on the road. Luckily there were no broken bones but as I looked up, dazed, at all the concerned faces looking down at me I recognised one of them: it was Joe Strummer from the punk band The Clash, come to check if I was okay.

I was taken to hospital suffering from shock and a bruised ego.

CHAPTER 5

Swanky Modes

I didn't want my art school days to end. I had just spent three years immersed in a creative, exciting, vibrant world, hanging out with brilliant people from diverse backgrounds. As far as I was concerned, I wanted this to be my life forever and funnily enough, it has turned out to be exactly that. Of course, back then, I didn't know if it was possible. I hadn't thought about careers, earning money or making plans for the future. Instead I focused on the last intense weeks of my course and helped my friend Willie Walters with her final collection, staying up all night to sew bugle beads onto her outfits.

I met Willie at St Martin's. In those days, St Martin's School of Art was a much smaller college than it is today and all the students from the different disciplines, Graphics, Fine Art, Fashion Design, etc., knew each other and socialised together. There was cross-college influence in terms of the work produced and frequent parties organised by the Students' Union. I was studying Graphic Design, Willie was on the Fashion Course and her boyfriend Ted was studying Sculpture on the celebrated and controversial 'A' Course directed by Peter Kardia. One of his fellow students, and a friend of ours, was Richard Deacon (later a Turner Prize winner). They worked with others on projects which have become legendary in terms of conceptual art education such as 'The Locked Room', 'The Hen Coop' critique and 'The Boxing Match' (part of Ted's practice), which we all attended. Fine Art students were the contestants, Anthony Caro and Gilbert & George gave the prizes and Ted acted as the MC. Willie had brought Mel Langer, an old school friend, along to see it and she was very upset because she thought that the boxing would be some sort of 'mime' but in fact they were genuinely going for it and some of them had blood running down their faces.

Willie's work was exceptional – her style, designs and fabric choices. For a moment, it made me question why I had never considered fashion as I had such a natural interest in it, but it had never occurred to me that I could choose Fashion as a course at art school. Anyway, I loved drawing so I knew I had made the right choice. Willie organised a fairground catwalk shoot of her collection (including a pet monkey) for her portfolio and our friend Niall McInerney (who went on to become an acclaimed fashion photographer), took the photographs. I modelled one of the pieces – a fitted, halterneck, shorts playsuit made in red satin. The fabric had been quilt-stitched to create padded hearts so the outfit had a theatrical structure to it. It was a great look – fun, sexy, strong and not for the faint-hearted. I teamed it with black leggings, thick wool socks and strappy heeled silver sandals. My long hair was poker-straight and I liberally applied dramatic shimmering blue eyeshadow before posing, hands on hips, looking directly into the camera.

I think it's an outfit that would shine just as brightly today.

Willie's friend Mel, who was tall and beautiful, was a sort of muse and would model the clothes that she made with the resulting photographs becoming part of Willie's application for St Martin's. Mel was, and still is, a brilliant organiser. It was really because of her that we got started at all. Just before we graduated, Mel called Willie to say there was a shop available at the end of her street in Camden and why didn't they take it and set something up. Willie was now married to her boyfriend Ted and had a baby. Even if she had wanted to take the conventional route in fashion it would have been hard for her because it meant moving to Hong Kong or Italy, where most fashion students went to find work. Besides, she knew it wouldn't fulfil her and the idea of doing something with Mel (who had a three-year-old boy by this point) was so much more exciting.

Willie and I had worked so well together, she invited me to join them. None of us could find the sort of clothes we wanted to wear on the high street so why not establish our own fashion brand and fill the sartorial gap? It was 1972 and we had been influenced by the rise of boutiques and inspired by the success of designers like Biba and Mister Freedom.

That this was an option was something that we took for granted, but in retrospect I realise that the viability of small-scale, independent designers with their innovative and quirky clothes was something very special and pretty much unique to London at that time. In many other cities around the world, such as Paris, Milan or New York, young designers like us would most likely end up in established fashion houses and businesses, conforming to the house style with a resultant stifling of innovation and experiment. In London, without realising it of course, the fashion world – and the worlds of art and music, come to think of it – followed Chairman Mao Zedong's dictum of 'let a hundred flowers bloom, and a hundred schools of thought contend'. The chairman had launched a campaign with the aim of encouraging new ideas in the arts and sciences in China and that's pretty much what was happening spontaneously all around us in London. All I mean by this tongue-in-cheek reference is that because of the opportunities there were in London for young designers and artists to do their own thing, there was a flowering diversity of ideas and approaches. In any case, we were part of our own very British Cultural Revolution, if just a tad different from what the chairman had in mind. If we were starting today, I don't know that we could pull it off. There is just as much creativity around as there ever was, of course, but everything seems much more corporate and what with the massive escalation in property prices in London, it's really difficult to afford premises. On the other hand, designers can just launch themselves on an unsuspecting world via the internet, but I do think that it was easier in our day.

We were brave, or foolhardy, depending on which way you wanted to look at it, but we never questioned what we were doing, even though we had no money or business experience. I mean, how hard could it be?! Well, very hard as it turns out, but that won't come as any surprise.

The premises Mel found had been a cobbler's at 193 Royal College Street, on the corner of Lyme Terrace and Royal College Street, NW1. She was living with Niall McInerney on Lyme Terrace at the time and spotted that the old cobbler had retired, leaving the tiny box-sized shop empty. Camden was the obvious place for us to be as Willie, Ted and our musician pal, John Grant, lived there already and we had lots of friends nearby, so this was a prominent place to display our clothes and distract shoppers from the humdrum high street alternatives. We each put £50 (today the equivalent would be around £577) into a pot to get our business off the ground.

Now we just needed a name, clothes to sell and customers to buy them – it was a big 'just'.

As a democratic collective it didn't work to use one of our names so we needed to think of something clever that captured who we were. The clothes shops of the fifties, the ones we grew up avoiding, always seemed to have the word 'mode' in the name and it had become an in-joke with us. We played around with this and talked about the

Irishwomen in Camden who would look at girls dressed in anything even slightly trendy or different and say, 'Ooh, she's swanky!' And that's how Swanky Modes was born. As a catchy, tongue-in-cheek name but with the utterly serious intention of offering something different in the fashion industry.

We started with Willie's graduation pieces – like the dress with fairy lights in the skirt and the hand-beaded full length dress – and the three of us also went to my parents' house in Surrey and made garments on their dining table. You might call it a capsule collection. We went fabric shopping on Berwick Street, Borovick Fabrics (established in Soho since 1932 and still going strong), a place called Theatreland on Soho Square and a shop in Kilburn that I used to ride past on my motorbike on the way to work. We picked up ends of lines, remnant stock and any vintage materials we could get enough of to make at least one piece. As luck would have it, my motorbiking boyfriend Phil's dad was a printer and although he had no connection with fashion or anything arty-farty, he came up with something really great for our logo. The logo he designed used graphics and lettering he already had and was a fifties line drawing of a woman's head with Swanky Modes in red text across the middle of it.

Very stylish and very swanky! He really hit the nail on the head.

Around this time, our friend Niall had decided to become a professional photographer. Having left Ireland at 17, he had a number of jobs, including lugging bags of potatoes up flights of stairs in high-rise buildings and selling them door to door. He ended up working for The Phoenix strip club in Soho, where he stood outside being charming and convincing people to come into the venue. The club owner, Billy Gardener, asked him to take pictures of the girls to display front of house so he went to see the photographer Lewis Morley, who had a studio on Greek Street. Lewis was a well-respected photographer (best-known for the iconic nude photo he took of Christine Keeler sitting on a chair), who helped Niall, lending him everything, all the equipment he needed, and showed him how to load the camera. He told Niall to bring the films back the following day and he would develop them for him – he was very generous and supportive of young talent. Niall knew this was his future so he left the Soho club scene behind. A year later, he heard that Billy, the owner of the club, had mysteriously drowned in his swimming pool.

To get started in the glamorous world of photography, Niall established a business – 'Piccadilly Press' – that in reality amounted to little more than a business card. He would photograph tourists in front of London landmarks before taking their contact details, rushing home to develop the pictures and then dashing straight to their hotel the following day in the hope they would buy them. A bit of a chancer, you're thinking? Well, he did what he had to do to get off the ground and it all worked out very well for him in the end, becoming a respected street photographer capturing shots of cool people in the city.

We asked Niall to shoot our first piece of publicity, which we had an unusual concept for. He took a series of photos of me getting undressed in a Swanky Modes outfit – stockings, a tight skirt and then a jacket. The idea would be like a striptease but in reverse. Then we gave the shots to my old boyfriend, Colin, who drew illustrations of them and we put them together to make a flicker book. It was very effective, like an animation – so it looked like the model was moving. At the time and probably to a certain extent even now, it was an innovative and memorable way of introducing our first season, catching the imagination of our customers, and the flicker book became our calling card. Niall also somewhat reluctantly shot our first collection in St Paul's churchyard in Covent Garden. He didn't see himself as a fashion photographer so he wasn't that interested. Ironically, he enjoyed it, he was good at it and that job was the beginning of an illustrious career as a catwalk photographer.

So we had a shop, an exclusive (more like limited!) collection, a strong work ethic and a shared vision. We had a steady stream of appreciative local customers too. It was a great start and yet we knew we had to do more. We couldn't rely on word of mouth or people finding us by accident, we had to be more press-savvy. Our first piece of publicity was in the London listings magazine, *Time Out*. I drew a fantastical illustration of a bird dressed in a Swanky Modes outfit and the text alongside it read:

Swanky Modes is a very small shop tucked away between Kings X and Camden Town. It's accessible from Kings X on the 46 bus route or use the BR (overland) to Camden Town Station or Camden Town tube and walk. It's a clothes shop run by three girls, two of whom studied design at art school – a lot of the more elaborate dresses (dresses that light up with fairly lights) were part of their diploma show. All their clothes are 'fun' clothes; they make everything themselves using old buttons, braiding and some materials that they've acquired from numerous jumble sales. They make fabulous rain jackets which are waist-length with a zipper front and elasticated cuffs, waistband and collar, and the main part of the jacket is made with shower curtain material. They fit both sexes and cost £2.95. They also make up the same design in satin and thick padded satin (£8). The rest of their clothes are modelled on 1950s gear and are only for girls. Shirred tops for wearing with jeans: £2.50; sleeveless day dresses between £4.50 and £5; 50s-style suits, straight skirt, fully lined and jacket with tucks and weird buttons; £11, incredible dresses, one with a skirt that lights up with fairy lights and with an embroidered story on the front, to order only; about £20. They hope to produce lots of very cheap funny garish clothes and also to design garments on commission. Go and see them, they're selling some of the greatest clothes around. Open 10–6, Mon–Sat.

It was a nice little piece but it wasn't going to transform our business. What we really needed was some professional PR help but we didn't even know what that was in those days. Mel and I thought we could take matters into our own hands so we got tarted up and took our clothes around to show magazine editors. In hindsight this was probably not how it was done but we had no idea how it all worked and as luck would have it, we caught the attention of one magazine.

Caroline Baker was the hugely respected fashion editor of *Nova*, a British glossy that *The Times* called a 'politically radical, beautifully designed, intellectual women's magazine'. This is exactly where we wanted to be. We took our clothes in to her and she immediately picked out our transparent rainwear. We had made a small range using shower curtain fabric (from 1950s remnant stock) both transparent and also printed; some with vanity mirrors, powder puffs and fish. Actually, we had always envisaged the plastic rainwear would be welded together as had been the cheap and cheerful macs of the 1950s – we had very carefully welded the samples together by hand using a soldering iron. I'm amazed that this worked, but it did quite effectively.

We designed batwing-sleeved jackets, trousers, circle skirts and coats to be worn over clothing as a top layer. One of the transparent coats featured a sealed pocket with 'debris' inside, which we found entertaining! The idea was both practical and commercial but also aimed to show the designs of both layers. The concept was an inversion of normality. Clothes usually conceal the body and hide detritus in the pockets from sight. Our transparent coats showed everything!

Caroline wanted the coat for the fashion pages in an upcoming issue of *Nova*, entitled 'April Showers'. She knew that the visionary, world-famous photographer Helmut Newton, who was doing the shoot, was on the lookout for macs so our selection fitted the brief. To ascertain his interest, she asked if we would do some drawings of the pieces that she could send to him so I sketched the macs with naked women underneath to show the detail of each transparent piece and because it was easier and less confusing than drawing them over other clothes. And this is exactly how he ended up shooting them: each model nude under their rainwear.

This was the big league, we felt excited and honoured!

But the nudity caused a bit of a rumpus within the walls of *Nova*. The editor of the magazine was not happy about running the photos but Caroline continued to fight her (and our) corner. While the debate was raging, publication was delayed and we had no idea if our see-through macs would ever hit the newsstands. We were fast running out of money and at exactly the wrong moment, the landlord of the shop ended our tenancy agreement. We were elbowed out because he decided to let to a massage parlour, which he clearly considered a better use of female talents than that we could offer and an all-round sounder business proposition.

Our business hung in the balance and we thought it could be over before it had really begun. Then *Nova* came out in spring 1973. Our rain mac collection was spread across four pages, fabulously styled and shot, each model starkers under our rainwear just as I had drawn them. Everything went mad. People wanted to know where they could buy these garments and what else we were planning and wholesale orders (which we had never had before) came in. This was the moment that really launched Swanky Modes.

So – hurrah! – we were back in business with orders coming in. But with no shop or even a workshop, we had no means of fulfilling them. Did we panic? Of course we did. There was nothing for it: we consulted the Yellow Pages directory of businesses. This dredged up a welding factory in an Islington backstreet so we hotfooted it around there to see what they could do for us: nothing, as it turned out. They looked askance at our complicated designs and guffawed at our paltry order quantities – minimum order 2,000.

We were shown the door.

We had to find another way of assembling our macs. Eventually we sewed the garments carefully, using tape to secure the seams and then a long stitch to stop the seams perforating and tearing apart.

At this point we were joined by a fourth partner, Judy Dewsbury, who had known Ted from Cheltenham College of Art and had just graduated from the Royal College, specialising in menswear. Ted had introduced her to Niall and Mel. Judy and Mel soon became good friends and Mel asked her to copy a much-loved brown tailored fifties coat in a bright pink Harris tweed with a pink velvet collar. The coat was exquisite and Mel still has it to this day. Judy was an expert pattern cutter and a kindred spirit so we invited her to join us at Swanky Modes and luckily for us, she agreed! It gave me the opportunity to learn from the best. So much of what I know about pattern cutting I learnt from working alongside Judy.

We were attempting to make up the orders following the *Nova* piece by working in Niall's house on Lyme Terrace. Unsurprisingly, he was getting rather fed up of us sewing at all hours at his kitchen table so we needed a new place – and fast. Yet again, Mel came up trumps and found a basement at 106 Camden Road, which became our workshop. A dignified old building with a stunning art nouveau glass frontage on the corner of the street, it was sandwiched between the public bar and the saloon bar of the Eagle Pub, which was on the corner of the terrace. It was fantastic and a bit rough as so many London boozers were back then before they got dolled up with gourmet menus and fancy furniture. The landlord, Aiden, was the same – tough, but lovely, an absolute treasure. We would go in to have a drink before we went off to parties, dressed outrageously, and nobody would bat an eyelid. There were several occasions of street brawls at chucking out time and our beautiful art nouveau windows bore the brunt of them twice. The first time we repaired the window with an expensive piece of curved glass but the second time we couldn't afford it so had to get a basic replacement instead.

Aiden became our hero one Saturday. I was in the shop when Judy arrived with her daughter Dora, who was a toddler then. We all sat on the raised platform in the shop when Judy spotted a pair of shoes at the bend of the stairs leading up to the kitchen. She said something like 'Who have you got upstairs?' and I said, 'That's strange, I thought I heard the shop bell go, but when I came up, there was nobody here.'

The shoes beat a silent retreat.

I immediately went next door to get Aiden, leaving Judy and Dora in the shop. Aiden came in and went straight upstairs, swiftly reappearing with a youth who he was holding by the neck of his clothes and asked us if we knew the intruder. Suddenly the boy reached backwards and grabbed a knife from his sock before dropping it on the floor. Judy and I were so shocked we didn't react for a moment, by which time the boy had grabbed the knife and stabbed Aiden in the leg before running out. Luckily, Aiden was made of stronger stuff so it didn't seem to worry him.

There were cellars from the basement that stretched out under the pavement. We hadn't been there long when we heard sweet tweeting sounds and assumed there must be a bird's nest tucked away somewhere. The reality was less cute when Nick, Judy's boyfriend, saw a rat scamper across the floor and realised the babies we could hear were rats and not birds. He went home and came back with his air rifle but in the end the problem was solved by the rat catcher's efficient Terrier and some disgusting poison.

It wasn't a glamorous atelier but we were happy.

I had the opportunity to buy a house in Royal College Street around this time too. It had a workshop downstairs and a flat above and I did consider it as I could have borrowed the deposit from my parents, but decided against it. That may have been a financial mistake, but as usual I wasn't thinking about material things ...

The documentary photographer Janette Beckman took a photo of us outside our shop. It looks like an album cover. Our faces are close together, looking straight to camera. What I see when I look at this photo now are not the early Punk hairstyles, the winged eye make-up or the enviable youth, I see four young women who built a successful business together without battling egos, big tantrums, bullying, sulking – or men. We were a true collective, an authentic collaboration where no single person claimed the credit for a decision or a design but instead gave the business the glory. The way we worked was a brilliant example of the whole being greater than the sum of the parts. We fed off each other and together developed results that none of us could have produced alone. It was wonderfully exhilarating. I think this is one of the reasons we were successful for so long and one of the things I am most proud of. That, and the fact there was no man involved in running the company.

How's that for girl power?

Of course we argued when things got tense. Usually this would be when we were stressed, in the middle of getting a collection ready to show to the buyers and press. There would be all-nighters when we would be working towards a deadline – finishing off samples, organising the show stand, pricing the garments. Often these were good-natured affairs, working together with our work experience students, laughing at ridiculous jokes the more tired we became, snacking and drinking coffee and keeping each other's spirits up. But sometimes tensions would build and one of the partners would explode. Then I can remember a few screaming rows, insults and equipment occasionally flying across the room – Mel once threw a sewing machine on the floor!

But that was as far as our arguments went. We always forgot about it the next day. Those girls could make me laugh myself silly. We all lived with each other in different formations at various times and genuinely just loved hanging out together. We had a shorthand Swanky Modes language we used, particularly when designing. For example, we adopted the word 'jocund' (meaning jolly and cheerful) as an insult to anything that looked too 'medieval'. If we thought something was jocund then we knew not to pursue it. Our tastes changed regularly but we always seemed to go in the same direction, very much a collective subconscious, so it was a harmonious process. We were generous to each other and pretty accurate with our predictions in fashion too. In fact, we were always one step ahead, which was great but also meant we would get bored before our customers did, so we would be pushing for what was next. Had we focused on our big hitters and continued to reproduce them, we would have been financially successful but terribly bored – and none of us did boring.

We spent a long time thinking about themes and being inspired by the world around us. It needed to be amusing or thought-provoking and to have a strong visual. Our 'Tonton Macoute' collection (S/S 1983) was a great example of this. The theme was based on a fantasy about a Caribbean island ruled by a despot who had suddenly left, taking his entourage with him. We imagined the rest of the islanders, thrilled at his departure, ransacking the palace and making fantastic outfits out of the jumble of clothes left behind: a mismatch of military fatigues and delicate floral tea gowns. The idea of this release from oppression resulting in the excitement of dressing up was something we loved.

Our usual way of working was to create toiles (a mock-up made in a cheaper fabric) of our designs first and then try them on ourselves. We were not worried about being rude to each other if the design didn't work, it was all part of the process and we needed honest feedback. I worked on a dress that stepped away from what we had been doing and adopted a Bauhaus style – a wide cut with diagonal fold and a large button – and the others hated it to begin with. They called it the 'penitential' garment or the 'prison warder' outfit and we all laughed about it, but I knew I could make it work, so after further adjustments it was one of our new shapes and an alternative to the figure-hugging look. It became a bestseller and we made it up in every colour.

After the excitement of *Nova*, we were on a roll. Not only were we fulfilling wholesale orders for the UK in department stores like Selfridges and Liberty (who found us at the trade shows we did) but we were also producing for Europe, the US and Australia as well. We continued with small runs of our designs for retail and collections and included quirky accessories made and sourced by Stephen Rothholz. Finding ends of runs of material and vintage fabrics was a constant occupation but we also stretched the boundaries of what was possible, even using car upholstery, and we were one of the first designers to use Lycra in anything other than sportswear. It was thrilling to see people queuing outside to come into our shop.

We showed our first seasonal collection in 1977 and ran two collections a year – Spring/Summer (S/S) and Autumn/Winter (A/W), each having a very distinctive narrative. The theme would be carried through every area of our work, including designing our own print too. One year we handscrawled Swanky Modes on silk in different colours and had bolts of fabric printed up that we transformed into leisurewear.

We were a small fashion house with a big attitude but we were largely ignored by the rest of the industry as we were not considered commercial high fashion. I don't think they appreciated our humorous, offbeat approach. The big glossy mags like *Vogue* didn't take much notice either until the eighties – they wanted American and European fashion houses – but we were often popping up in *19*, *Ritz* (three pages of the model Marie Helvin in Swanky Modes, taken by David Bailey), *Boulevard*, *Nova* and the *Sunday Times Magazine*. *ID* and *The Face* loved us too, which gives you an idea of the sort of following we had and it was great to get the recognition.

In 1978 we took part in the Individual Clothes Show, a trade show featuring a collective of small designers not included in the larger wholesale events. It was organised by Cath Knox and Wendy Booth and they invited designers who they thought were exciting. This coincided with our new collection using nylon Lycra – we had been looking for a fabric that had a two-way stretch so we could create designs that moved comfortably with the body.

Creatively it was exciting, working with a new fabric. It was impossible to flat pattern cut and we had to do what the fabric wanted rather than impose our will on it. As we did not have a four-thread machine (which is how stretch fabrics are sewn today), we made the garments on a flat-bed straight stitch machine. We had to carefully stretch the fabric when sewing the side seams and use a method of binding to tighten the edges, e.g.

the 'slashes' that diagonally held the bust in shape with the 'Slasher' dress.

The designs looked stunning on the body but had absolutely no hanger appeal due to the floppy nature of the fabric so we hit on the idea of showing the garments on body forms cut from sheet plastic. We also started producing a 'look book' of photos, which we displayed on our stand. From then on, until the mid-eighties, our photos were beautifully styled by our friend Susie Slack. At that first Individual Clothes Show our model Gemma would be sent to get a coffee wearing a Lycra dress and return with a trail of future buyers. They were a big hit, especially as they coincided with the explosion of Disco.

⊗ ⊗ ⊗

The inimitable singer Grace Jones gave a newspaper interview to promote her upcoming album *Portfolio*. The male journalist who interviewed her seemed to swing between awe and shock as she joined him for lunch with a large appetite and wielding a whip. He accused her of scaring the waiters and didn't know what to make of her producing a cassette player and singing him her latest song. By the time they got to the fashion shoot he seemed overwhelmed by her brilliant, unique power but luckily for us, he captured the moment when she was shown what she would be wearing for the photo:

Then she sees the dress – a tight Lycra creation, taut as a drum. She screams. She loves it. Once inside she undulates cross the studio floor like a panther, a snake – a snake who sips champagne and departs in a limousine.

The dress was ours – black Lycra jersey with padlocks and chains. It also came in red, turquoise and then, later on, yellow. We had designed a range of Lycra Disco dresses for our S/S 1978 'Graffiti' collection and continued to produce them well into the eighties. As one of the first fashion houses to use the stretchy Lycra fabric for anything other than swimwear, the dresses were a triumph and very popular on dance floors globally. We made them in black and primary colours, which worked perfectly for the bodycon silhouette and called them the 'Strangler', 'Flasher', 'Amorphous' and 'Geo' (short for geometric). The 'Amorphous' dress, more of a sculpture than a dress, has been on show at the V&A Museum. We draped the Lycra on a stand and then cut into sections of the fabric so when it was laid out it looked a little like an amoeba, hence the name.

This dress became so popular that it almost had a media life of its own. We even made one specially for Dame Edna's appearance on BBC1's *Top of the Pops*, singing her hit song 'Disco Matilda'. Best of all, a customer bought it from us and took it to New York, where she wore it out one evening. As she came into the restaurant and took off her coat, people clapped! She came in and told us about it when she got back.

The dress Grace Jones wore from the collection was called the 'Padlock' dress and she looked sensational in it – we couldn't have asked for a better model. That dress is now in the Museum of London.

We did receive a bit of a backlash from feminists arguing that we were making clothes that women wore for men, not for themselves, and that they were too sexual. We certainly were glorifying the female form but for the woman herself, not for the benefit of anyone else. These were liberating clothes. It was about reclaiming our own bodies and nobody else's business, plus they were comfortable to wear and easy to dance in. Women felt powerful, sexy and relaxed in them – quite a feat to expect from one dress.

In 1972 the sculptor and performer Andrew Logan established The Alternative Miss World – a fancy dress competition inspired by Crufts, the annual dog show organised by The Kennel Club – described as a 'pansexual beauty pageant' and took the format of the Miss World competition. What started in his flat became a big event over the years staged in various London locations. The format was similar to a beauty parade, where the competitors had to wear three different outfits – daywear, eveningwear and swimwear – and remember that 'bizarre was beautiful'. They paraded in front of a line-up of famous judges and Andrew, dressed half as a woman and half as a man, was the Master of Ceremonies, with co-hosts like Divine, Grayson Perry, Ruby Wax and Julian Clary. The early days were captured on camera by the film-maker, artist and gay activist Derek Jarman, who also won the event in 1975 as Miss Crepe Suzette.

We took part the year Derek was filming and appeared in the documentary, *The Alternative Miss World*. We were backing singers for the make-up artist Yvonne Gold, even though none of us could really sing but boy, did we look amazing! The compère, the inimitable drag queen Divine, declared us his daughters as we were like mini versions of him and the audience gasped when we came out. Yvonne was wearing a huge blonde wig and a skin-tight sexy catsuit. As we belted out 'Hey Big Spender', we danced around in our own designed jumpsuits made of black nylon Lycra with chains and conical bras – or 'torpedo tits' as we called them (about 15 years before Jean Paul Gaultier designed them for Madonna). Judy was pregnant at the time but still managed to stay upright on gold stiletto sandals.

When I say none of us could sing, that wasn't strictly true, one of us could. As well as the Swanky Modes four, we were joined by our assistant Anne Martin. When Anne wasn't working with us, she was the singer Bette Bright and was part of the band Deaf School as well as a performer in her own right. Introduced to us through the fashion pages of *Nova*, she had visited the shop to buy clothes to wear onstage. She would pop in to see what we had been working on and Clive Langer, the guitarist from Deaf School, would come with her. This was how Clive met Mel and they began dating.

Anne started to work for us when she wasn't gigging and immediately became one of the family. She remembers Swanky Modes as being 'utterly fabulous, a creative hub of wonderfulness'. At one point she moved into my brother Chris' flat for a while. He was renting from an old Jewish lady in Kilburn, Mrs Harrington, who he kept an eye on as she was suffering from dementia. She came up with some rather bizarre tales, once telling him that she was to be married to a man that she'd just met in a sandwich bar in the Tottenham Court Road, but had unfortunately mislaid his address! Doris Lessing, who later won a Nobel Prize for Literature, lived immediately next door and used to pop in to see how Mrs Harrington was getting on and once remarked it was rather wonderful how the human mind managed to conjure up whatever it needed.

When Derek Jarman's documentary came out in 1980, we were invited to the premiere. We dressed in Dolly Parton-inspired outfits, our partners dressed as cowboys and we hired a white limousine to pick us up from outside the shop. Anne had just broken up with the lead singer of Deaf School, Steve Allen, and was staying with Mel and Clive in the flat above Swanky Modes. Mel thought we should find her a cowboy for the evening. Clive had left the band by this point and had become a record producer, working with an up-and-coming band called Madness. They sound fun, we thought. Mel said they were, especially the lead singer Suggs, who she thought would be up for dressing as a cowboy. It turned out he was a big fan of Bette Bright and was keen to meet her so Mel invited him along and he entered into the crazy spirit of the evening. When we all got back to the shop in the early hours, we realised, in our excitement to leave, that nobody had brought a door key with them. We were locked out and standing on the pavement in outrageous party outfits unsure of what to do next when Suggs, still dressed as a cowboy, started to shimmy up the drainpipe. We watched in awe as he reached the first-floor window and managed to open it and climb in before coming down to open the door.

Our hero! Anne certainly thought so.

After their first date with us all, Anne and Suggs continued to see each other and several years later, they were married. Of course, Swanky Modes designed and made the wedding outfits. Anne wanted a Russian-style Anna Karenina theme so we made her a white leather jacket, corset top and a big hooped skirt. She finished the fabulous look with a white fur Cossack hat. Willie's daughter, Tamsin, and Mel's daughter, Isla, were bridesmaids and had matching Cossack hats and white fur muffs, while Matthew, the son of Madness guitarist Chris Foreman, was a pageboy in velvet knickerbockers and buckled shoes. It was a few days before Christmas and utterly magical, particularly as it snowed the night before the wedding so London was at a peaceful, festive standstill.

Firmly ensconced in the fashion industry, we had won the respect of many of our contemporaries like Vivienne Westwood and Malcolm McLaren, who popped over to see us one day. Their shop had been through several transformations already and they were unsure what to do next but they were angling to find out our direction. We kept our cards close to our chest. They renamed their premises SEX, Punk exploded in the UK and they created the most incredible movement. Vivienne and Malcolm were part of the stage line-up at the ICA (Institute of Contemporary Arts) in 1975, where we were also invited to take part in a fashion forum, but we felt uncomfortable about the format. Instead we produced a short show for the night called 'Crime of Passion Fashion' with a storyline about someone going around murdering people who were wearing Swanky Modes. Our friends, family and models and even some of our customers – Connie, Lynne and Shirley-Anne – took part and wore our designs. Richard Deacon played the part of a shady character and there was even a body builder from Greece!

My three brothers all took part as well, in a scene where they were waving the Olympic flag, more or less in unison. Jeremy, the baby of the family, first started getting to know my life with Swanky Modes when he was 19 and found it very exotic and thrilling. He took a year off before going to university and when he came back, he visited us in the shop and we all asked him about his adventures. He revealed that he had had a fling with an older woman while travelling.

'Ooh, tell us about her,' said Mel.

Jeremy revealed that her name was Val and she was 30.

'Well, we're nearly 30,' said Mel.

Uh-oh, Jeremy must have thought, *I've put my foot in it here.*

'But you all seem so young and vibrant and exciting to me,' he said.

'Good recovery, Jeremy,' said Judy laconically.

My family have always been very important to me and it was nice to see Jeremy growing up and sharing his experiences and adventures with me.

⊗ ⊗ ⊗

We took a creative approach to everything we did and loved to surprise people. Encouraged by the reception we got at the ICA, we decided to do something similar for an upcoming catwalk show. We also wanted to say goodbye to the old decade and welcome the eighties by celebrating our retrospective designs and showcasing our new collection.

What better way to do that than with a musical?

Yes, exactly what we thought.

We actually thought about it for a long time. It's how

we worked, chatting about stuff until it was almost too late and then working to a strict deadline. We had just six weeks to put together our Swanky Extravaganza, which we titled 'Seams Like A Dream' and staged at the Notre Dame Hall in Soho in 1980. We called our pal Greg Cruikshank, who had produced our first show at the ICA, and paid for him to fly back from San Francisco, where he was living. He was part of The Cockettes, a hippy and hedonistic theatre group based over there. They all lived together, commune-style, and would stage shows with costumes picked up from the old MGM Studios. The founder, Hibiscus, an actor and performance artist, objected to the group becoming too commercial so he split off and formed the Angels of Light, performing free shows. He was to be one of the first to be claimed by AIDS in 1982. Greg was our brilliantly flamboyant narrator and choreographed the show too.

We had no budget after we had paid Greg's flight but everyone happily gave their services for free and we worked with the most wonderful people who, if they hadn't been pals before the show, were firm friends after it. They were an eclectic bunch who worked with us – artists who designed and painted the set, like Ben Kelly, Duggie Fields and Andrew Logan, musicians like Glen Matlock (ex-Sex Pistols), who played with his band The Spectres, models who worked for us in return for clothes and usherettes including the then unheard-of Boy George. The backing singers were our fabulous male friends like our pal Jerry

Kingett, Stephen Rothholz, celebrity hairstylist Keith Wainwright, my old boyfriend Colin, and Ted, Willie's husband, who formed a Greek chorus and sang, 'If you want some hanky-panky, come to where the modes are swanky.' We had spotted the actress and singer Eve Ferret at a New Year's Eve party, looking amazing in one of our dresses so we invited her to sing a number at the show and she did. We also asked Cliff, our trimming salesman if he wanted to come and sing too. That's not as crazy as it sounds because we had found out he had had an illustrious pop career with his band Cliff Bennett and The Rebel Rousers (they had a big hit with 'Got To Get You Into My Life', written and produced by Paul McCartney). He came out of retirement just for us and sang 'I Can't Stand The Rain' before going back to his day job. One of our stylist friends introduced me to Mervyn, who was a furniture maker and helped with the set, and some time later became my boyfriend.

Rehearsing the musical was tricky because we were relying on goodwill but we managed to cobble together about four weeks of rehearsals and worked late nights on the outfits in between. To add a further level of stress, we were being filmed by Mike Southon for the BBC's *Arena* documentary. They were doing a programme taking an offbeat look at fashion or maybe that should have been a look at offbeat fashion! We had a camera crew with us and they documented the few days running up to the musical and the musical itself. It's incredible to watch it now and see us, bustling around in the workshop, sewing machines whirring, answering the phone, discussing fabrics and eating cake with a small child toddling over our patterns on the cutting table. Strangely enough, Mike is now a friend and collaborator of my baby brother Jeremy – I met him again years later through that connection.

It was utter madness to launch the new collection in such an unusual way, not least because of the amount of work involved, but it caught everyone's imagination and there was an industry buzz about us. We wanted the show to be fun, full of amateur dramatics and also give a tongue-in-cheek look at the world of fashion. The idea was to parody a conventional catwalk show and laugh at the way we all praised and worshipped at the fashion monolith. We made a fake monument with our name, Swanky Modes, on it and we dressed as cavewomen and brought it on (with a nod to Stanley Kubrick's *2001: A Space Odyssey*) at the beginning of the production. The finale was a catwalk show where the models came out in the new collection, each carrying a beautifully mirrored letter sculpted by Andrew Logan that they stuck in a giant book at the back of the stage. After the last model had walked, it spelt out SWANKY MODES.

As we say in the documentary, if we had been in the rag trade we would have given up and gone and baked bread or run a sweet shop instead. But we weren't in it for the money or running a business – none of us were interested in that – we were four designers driven by the desire to create. The show was incredible and totally over the top. And we organised a retrospective exhibition at the Angela Flowers Gallery which was then on Tottenham Mews to complement the *Arena* programme. We were exhausted but thrilled that such a great team effort had made something so wonderful. At the end of the show we realised someone had nicked the petty cash. Years later, I was reading an interview with Boy George, who was talking about his early poverty-stricken years living in squats and how he would occasionally nick money from jobs he was working on.

I wonder if that's where our cash went? I hope so.

Around this time, Phil and I were coming to the end of our relationship although I think I realised this before he did. I was surrounded by friends getting married and having children. When Willie and Ted got married in 1971, they had a horse and cart to take them to Camden Town Hall for the ceremony and then we all had a big party. I partied a bit too hard and Willie had to nip out of her wedding reception to take me home. I was very happy for them but I knew it wasn't what I yearned for. My friends didn't try to persuade me otherwise, there was no pressure to change my mind and I half expected I might, but I didn't and I haven't. We just celebrated Willie and Ted's 50th wedding anniversary so it was the right decision for them.

Much of the seventies was one big social. The flat above the shop was our hub, with people constantly popping in, using it as a second workshop, partying, eating and hanging out. We would often throw impromptu gatherings and meet lots of new people who happened to pop by with others we knew, like the night when The Sex Pistols turned up without incident (unusually). There was a real sense of a creative community and we always celebrated each other's wins and commiserated over the failures.

At another party we had a special performance from a client of ours. A stripper, she would regularly ask us to design outfits for her. She asked me to make her a circle skirt and there was so much fabric, I had to lay it out on the floor of the shop to work on it. I made a mistake on the overlocker and ripped a hole in it but it was covered in ruffles so I patched it and she never noticed. One day she popped in and we mentioned we were having a party that night and she was welcome to come for a drink. She said she would love to and asked us if we wanted her 'to do my thing'. Believe it or not, we were incredibly naïve, we had never been to a strip show and we said sure, thinking it would be a bit of fun. A burlesque tease maybe, something coy and demure. Instead it was a full-on, in-your-face strip and it went down rather badly – we were all speechless.

Wherever we went, we went as a posse of four or eight as our partners came too, piling into a van and heading out. Often we would make outfits for the event we were going to, which could be a bit distracting from the day job. It would take us ages to get ready and that was part of the fun of the evening. If there was a theme, we were all over it. We once went to a science fiction party as the Junior Anti-Sex League (characters from the novel *1984*), dressed in bottle green scrubs I had made, with swimcaps to make us look bald and lobotomy scars made from Copydex rubber cement – and nipped to the pub first for a quick drink! Our party outfits were often more shocking than stylish and the boys were always happy to follow suit. It was incredibly gender fluid and we all wore make-up, glitter, jewels around our eyes and big Afro wigs of silver foil with eyelashes to match.

We were never low-key.

I think we must have been a pain in the arse to invite over because although we may have thought we brought the party with us, we also brought the music. We would bring tapes of our favourites, including sixties Soul, Funk and old R&B, and switch off whatever was playing in favour of our playlist. Maybe we were a bit of a nightmare but I'm going to blame the arrogance of youth and the safety of being in a group.

Music has always been a big part of my life and there was a running soundtrack throughout the Swanky Modes years. We saw Tina Turner at the Shepherds Bush Odeon, Bob Marley at the Lyceum, Kid Creole, Prince, The Clash at Finsbury Park and Kilburn and the High Roads, Ian Dury's first band. We saw Debbie Harry and Wayne/Jane County at Dingwalls Dance Hall in Camden. Dingwalls was a favourite music venue in the seventies and if I didn't have anyone to dance with, I would dance my way around one of the columns holding up the roof. The whole Camden Lock market area grew up around it.

Ian Dury's bass player Humphrey Ocean was at school with my brothers and we were all friends. I had tickets for Al Green, but for the first performance, and the rest of the girls had tickets for the second, so at the end of the show I hid in the lavs and came out just before the second show began. The band were sitting on the stage and I suddenly felt rather embarrassed so I asked them if they wanted a drink and then thought, *Shit, can I afford it?* We were fans of Hank Wangford too, both his music and his medical ability. He was a rock star and also a gynaecologist, based at The Hospital for Women on Soho Square, so we all went to him for birth control and women's health issues.

There are so many parties I don't remember but one I won't forget was thrown by Derek Jarman in Charing Cross, in what was really a glorified coal hole. We went down a dark tunnel which opened out onto a large vaulted ceiling space with a screen at the far end. I was told not to go beyond it as I watched men disappear discreetly behind the screen!

We loved an out-of-town party and would head off in our van to wherever we were invited. My youngest brother, Jeremy, was now at Oxford University and he invited several of us to come to Sunday formal dinner at his college, St Edmund Hall. We turned up and fell out of the van, looking glamorous and outrageous, and attracted quite a bit of interest from the students as he showed us around the college.

At formal dinner, the students all wear their gowns and the professors sit at the top table on a raised section. Each student could apply for two guest tickets to formal dinner each term, so Jeremy had been calling in favours and negotiating for several weeks to get the extra tickets for us. As we entered and went to our table there was a ripple of noise and quite a few turned heads. We were sitting with him and some of his friends just below the top table, in the centre of the hall, and caused quite a stir with our outfits and appearance, particularly Bette Bright, whose hair was bright red then. We had a great time and afterwards, Jeremy told me that the Vice Principal had approached him the next day and asked, 'Mr Young, who were your guests at dinner last night?'

There were several trips to the Southwest too, including Bath and Bristol. After one party somewhere in a field in Somerset, Mel and I were cosy in bed in the back of the van when the back doors flew open and a guy from the party climbed in. We both tensed, uncertain what was to happen next. After clambering over us and into the front seat, he let himself out of the passenger door. He never said a word!

Dinner parties were a big thing. Not posh ones, just evenings where everyone cooked and guests brought food to add to the table. We lit lots of candles and would often make an installation out of the food. There was nothing like styling a long dinner table before everyone arrived and it was gradually wrecked during the evening. Who can forget the pie made of pastry in the shape of a penis?! I do forget what the filling was, though.

Set dressing was a passion, whether it was for a dinner, a party, a catwalk or the windows of the shop. For the Queen's Silver Jubilee, we put a lifesize cutout of her waving in the window and then for the wedding of Prince Charles and Lady Diana, their cutouts were mechanised so it looked like Charles was putting a ring on Diana's finger. At Christmas we set up the entire Nativity and replaced the faces of the shepherds and the kings with illustrations of our suppliers. A great artist friend of ours, Archie, painted them – he earned a very good living painting copies of Old Masters so he was the perfect person for the job.

Swanky Modes did really well throughout the second half of the seventies, helped in part by the high-profile characters who were wearing our designs. We were regularly contacted by people in the music and film businesses to dress or design for stars. Midge Ure's manager got in touch to ask if we would design a baseball-inspired collection for Midge's first band, Slik. We took that idea and worked on a collection with cutout lettering that created a positive negative effect, producing trousers, tops and dresses.

For another collection, we designed fabric with a thumbprint and a phone number underneath it as a tongue-in-cheek nod to police arrest. The number was ours and we thought it was rather a fun form of marketing. We made various items in it and the pop star Toyah bought a pair of trousers, which she was photographed in. Then we started to receive rude phone calls from strange men. It didn't upset us, we would just answer and say to each other, 'Come and listen, it's the wanker again!'

It soon stopped.

As much as we attracted the good and the great, we also appealed to the weird and wonderful and not-so-wonderful. In our first shop there was a screen and a man used to come in and start wanking behind it in full view of us. Then we had the chap dressed head-to-toe in red and black rubber with a cape and a pump that he gave a quick press on for air. He looked like a superhero – although not one you might want to be saved by. I think he may have mistaken us for a fetish fashion brand. As did the guy who came in asking if we did made-to-measure. I was on my own in the shop and I said we did and he wondered if we had more of the transparent lurex fabric and if I would drape it over him. I went out to the workshop and came back in with a roll to find him standing naked in the middle of the shop. History erases what I may have said to him, but it won't have been pretty!

I did occasionally wonder what people made of us, particularly when the police turned up as part of Operation Julie, a drug bust. They assumed as we were a 'bohemian shop selling outrageous clothes', we might know something. Mel was in the shop and they came in to ask about a girl we knew whose boyfriend appeared to be caught up in the dodgy dealings. They had broken their door down and he made a run for it, jumping over a wall in just his pants and getting away. Now they were gathering evidence. Mel said she wasn't sure that she did know the girl and that she would ask us so she came down to the basement where we were in the workshop and said, 'The police are here and I don't know what to say.' What she hadn't realised was that the copper had followed her down. I think he was a bit cross, but he didn't pursue his line of questioning.

We did think about getting a shop on Conduit Street in Mayfair, somewhere more central and possibly less of a beacon to sleaze, but we didn't have enough money so contemplated taking investment. There was a Greek chap called Aristos Constantinou, who owned a fashion brand, Ariella. He lived in a fancy place on The Bishops Avenue, N2, with his pretty, young wife, Elena. A big name in retail, he drove a hard bargain, pushing for 51 per cent of the business, to which we said no as he would then own Swanky Modes. We were on good terms so there could have been a deal to be done further down the line but six months later, he was shot dead by a silver gun at his house on New Year's Day. It was thought he had disturbed a burglary but there are various conspiracy theories surrounding his murder.

Swanky Modes:
The Collections

FOR THOSE OF you who would like to delve a little deeper into our archive, here's a list of our collections. It is written here with the caveat that it is not complete or definitive, but as much as the four of us can remember. What we particularly loved about each collection was how we themed it and you will see from some how much fun we had – this shone out of every catwalk show.

1972

We sourced the most fabulous materials from unusual places, including second-hand wholesale outlets and jumble sales, unearthing vintage chintz drapes, car upholstery and even shower curtain fabric. The latter were fifties prints with names like 'boudoir' and 'bamboo' and we transformed them into rain macs, batwing sleeve tops, tracksuit-style trousers, circle skirts and bomber jackets that could be worn over clothes. Very practical! These were the garments featured in *Nova* magazine. There were outfits in lamé, satin, net and tinsel, which we made as samples, popped on the rail or in the window of our first shop and then customers could have a bespoke garment made. We made a dress covered with elegant handwritten, very rude, graffiti that created the overall effect of a floral print and experimented with the trompe l'oeil style – making a dress which included the body of the wearer, for men and women, featuring muscles, hair chest, cleavage and jewellery.

1973

By now, we had moved to the shop at 106 Camden Road and continued to experiment with a variety of styles and one-off designs available for made-to-measure. There was a standout green glitter 'monster' tracksuit worn by the Australian actress, Little Nell. We continued to be led by the fabrics we found and a mix of styles which took our fancy. It was a difficult start to the year because of the three-day week when there was a restriction to working hours. It was imposed by the Conservative government in response to the industrial action by coal miners and rail workers. The idea was to save electricity and the ruling lasted for several months.

1974

Along with our made-to-measure pieces, we curated interesting accessories in the shop with a particular penchant for fifties earrings and talc tins with African designs from Stephen Rothholz. There were dresses and playsuits in polka dots, leather jackets and miniskirts with diamanté trim and lace-sided dresses and jumpsuits. The sheer net and sparkly satin tulle were exactly the thing for a party but the most offbeat decision was the leopard print all-in-ones made from car seat material! We just designed outfits as they occurred to us, organically changing and not yet restricted to seasonal collections.

1975

The year of our ICA performance 'Crimes of Passion Fashion'. We designed dresses in black 'wet look' fabric that stretched one way, with cutouts filled in with clear plastic and custom-made T-shirts with names in plastic cutout. There were fluorescent plastic slim trousers and 'wire insulating' tube finishes, using big stitches to decorate a sleeve hem or neckline.

1976

The year of gorgeous clashing colours – orange, lime, hot pink – and plastic orange and fluorescent green trousers. We fell in love with towelling fabric and candlewick too, more usually used for bedspreads. There was overlocking on the outside of garments and large button details down the side of slim dresses or on a shoulder. At Christmas, we made transparent stockings and stuffed them with beauty treats like nail varnish.

1977

We started wholesale, which was a big step for us. We made daywear in cotton, using contrast binding on jackets, trousers and shorts. There were airtex frills, more big buttons and the word 'Swanky' across the backsides (as photographed by Mike Berkovsky). Most importantly, we designed our first collection using nylon Lycra, a fabric previously used in the UK only for swimwear, which gave a two-way stretch. It was available in black and primary colours, which worked well for the bodycon silhouettes of the S/S 78 'Graffiti' collection.

1978

We shared our first collection publicly, taking part in the Individual Clothes Show at the Athenaeum Hotel, with a group of other young designers including Chrissie Walsh, Ian Batten and Fred Spurr. We showed off our stretch Lycra designs on shapes cut out in rigid plastic because they had no hanger appeal – they were floppy until worn. This was also one of the reasons we did our own photo sessions for our collections because we wanted to demonstrate them to their best advantage. The dresses were called 'The Flasher', 'Amorphous', 'The Padlock', 'The Slasher', 'Geo' and 'The Strangler'. We designed a graffiti print which was painted onto silk and cotton and used linen and shirting weight cotton too. We also made pyjamas from the graffiti print silk and paired them with a black bra, inspired by the silk pyjamas I had bought at a jumble sale and wore to parties with a black bra underneath. The colour palette was red, yellow, turquoise, black and white. Our A/W collection included corduroy and a tyre track print too.

1979

The S/S collection focused again on nylon Lycra, a finger print, cotton and silk and the A/W collection was the first we named. It was called the 'Tony Rome' after the Frank Sinatra film of the same name, in which he plays a private investigator in Miami. Two of the signature garments were a pleat-fronted miniskirt and jackets for both men and women with big shoulders, predating the eighties shoulder pad. The inside lining of the jacket was the tyre print silk. We also worked with a houndstooth check, black PVC and wool and the lead colour was royal purple – a shade we called 'bruise', which tied in with the gangster theme of royal blue, bottle green and of course, black.

1980

'Seams Like A Dream' was our musical show – staged at the Notre Dame Hall and filmed by the BBC's *Arena* – which doubled as a retrospective and new collection catwalk show. We premiered the 'Paco' collection of cotton piqué, checked madras, taffeta and power net in scarlet, blue, white and black. At the trade show that year we were amazed to see other brands using Lycra in lurid, clashing colours – they had jumped on our bandwagon just as we had jumped off it. Bored with the Lycra look, we were ready for something new. Our A/W collection was full of black lace and taffeta in orange and moss green and lots of mohair in royal blue and turquoise and a divine oatmeal/grey/red bobble tweed. The HUGE jewellery was designed by Stephen Rothholz and inspired by washboards used by musicians in the 1920s, and some of it was incorporated into the yokes of dresses or as a geometric shape on the décolletage or back.

There was a magazine piece entitled 'If You Go Down to the Woods Today' which said of us…

An individual theme to emerge from several go-ahead young British designer collections this winter is one reminiscent of medieval times, of Robin Hood. The clothes have a theatrical feel to them and come in wools, felts, mohair and soft suede made up in lovely rich colours – violets, greens, turquoise and peat brown. Although at present this look will appeal to an adventurous minority, we feel that it will soon find its way (albeit in diluted form) into stores and high street shops …

1981

The S/S collection was a wonderful mix of tartan and lace for dresses, oversize jackets, slim trousers and cocktail looks. We called them 'chocolate box styles'. There was more lace in the A/W collection as well as lamé damask in gold and either pale blue, black or pale pink and a Picasso print handpainted on wool, cotton and taffeta. The cocktail theme continued with dresses and sixties-inspired slim slacks, gymslip dresses over blouses, leather and lace bustiers and wide taffeta trousers handpainted in gold.

1982

The 'Fijian' collection for S/S adopted a new material – raffia – as well as cotton and silk. The raffia was sourced from The Shell Shop, where I used to work when I was a student at St Martin's, and we showcased the look on our ill-fated Riverside TV appearance. We made up a running man print, championed sports styles and produced swimwear in polycotton Lycra and raffia too. The colour palette was sea blue, russet red, cream and turquoise.

The A/W season was the 'Russian' collection and featured wool, faux leather, faux fur and jersey with trims, including vintage beads in various colour combinations and tassels. The central colours were black, red and grey.

1983

The unforgettable 'Ton Ton Macoute' S/S collection in cotton, cotton drill, cotton Lycra and silk, with webbing, D-ring buckles and a pink and turquoise flower print in khaki, navy, cream and pink. For A/W, we went 'Secret Agent', with wool jersey, cotton and mohair and used school-style raincoat fabric. There was also wool, silk and organza and the colours were predominantly black, royal blue, aubergine, moss green and crimson. We took part in a Milan trade show 'Milano Vende Moda' and also won a prize for London Fashion Week Twilight Zone, with young, trendsetting eveningwear. We were also asked to design an outfit each for Snoopy and Belle for *Snoopy In Fashion* – a prestigious fashion exhibition at the Seibu Art Forum in Tokyo.

1984

After the cut and thrust of military and spywear, we took an about turn and designed a 'Country Garden' collection for S/S, full of satinised cotton, cotton tulle and cotton Lycra as well as sporty swimwear with elasticated straps. Jade, cornflower blue, violet and white were the lead colours. Nick Knight did a fantastic shoot of the collection. This led nicely into the 'Victorian Narrative' collection for A/W, with wool jersey, checked wool daywear, black and white houndstooth, trousers with turn-ups, elasticated braces and bejewelled shoulder straps with flashes of scarlet throughout.

1985

The year we started doing mid-season collections and had the 'Happy Valley' in S/S. There was oatmeal Moygashel fabric, birdseye check cotton Lycra, cotton Lycra rib and silk chiffon. We used a cotton damask sprigged with tiny flowers and this dyed very well in many shades – it was an underwear fabric called 'Squire Bowker'. Lots of large wooden buttons and the colour palette was cornflower blue, tea rose, white, oatmeal and hot pink. A/W mid-season was the 'Medieval' collection in black, grey, ochre and a marbled print in purple, mustard and gold, with heavy stretch cotton jersey, cotton Lycra rib and black panne velvet. The main season was 'Vintage Skiing in China', using corduroy, heavy cotton jersey, rib, silk organza and panne velvet in khaki, russet, black and fuchsia. We designed a black swimsuit with ripple skirt, which was sold in Liberty alongside other pieces.

1986

The S/S collection was 'World Badge Hiking', using a globe badge on garments and accessories, with chocolate brown, orange, white, blue and green colourways. We used airtex, cotton Lycra rib, cotton Lycra and stretch denim. Our 'Electric Print' collection for A/W was a return to corduroy, wool jersey and lots of zips in deep crimson, jade and navy.

1987

We stopped the shows and started selling through an agent. S/S was focused on peasant shapes, with cotton jersey, lace, broderie anglaise and gathered fabric. For A/W, we used a pleated lamé, silk, cotton jersey and forties-style 'goddess' swimwear in cotton Lycra, with a colour palette of cream, navy, brown, black, sunshine yellow and red and gold fine-weight lamé. *Vogue* featured the actress Brigitte Nielsen wearing our two-piece with strapless buttoned top in black Lycra grosgrain. We made a black PVC jacket lined in red for the musician Toyah Wilcox too.

1988

As we were selling through an agent, the process became more organic rather than focusing on seasons, but we did a summer collection using Indian and African print fabrics. I forget the name of this collection but we made shirts, cardigans, dresses, trousers and shorts. In fact I had shorts and I made an identical pair for Isla to wear when we went camping.

1990/91

This collection was named 'The Silent Three', inspired by a story about schoolgirls, which appeared in the fifties comic, *School Friend*. We made jumpsuits with hoods and layered the outfit with shorts and miniskirts using cotton Lycra, PVC and panne velvet in black, cream, grey and mauve. Judy's sister, Sarah, did comic drawings, which we used for publicity purposes.

1992/93

Our final collection featured men's and women's swimwear and we printed up postcards with a drawing of Greek male and female statues wearing our designs. We also designed Lycra dresses based on our original successes, changing the style slightly and using different weighted fabric. One of these dresses was worn by Rachael Fleming in the *Trainspotting* film (1996). There were see-through chaps and fitted jackets too, using a heavier weighted transparent fabric than we had for our early rainwear collection. The cut was interesting and came from one I had developed for the jumpsuit pattern – I wore one of the jackets at our closing-down party.

CHAPTER 6

Reasons To Be Cheerful

I think we may have been at the height of our powers in the early eighties. The big, old-fashioned dial telephone in the workshop didn't stop ringing. One day it was the producer of BBC2's *Riverside* – a weekly magazine programme about popular culture – inviting us on to talk about Swanky Modes. After our success with *Arena*, we thought it might be fun to do a live interview show so we said, 'Oh, go on then' and spent some time on our outfits, incorporating elements from our latest collection, 'Raffia'. Had we known we would be appearing with the controversial post-Punk band Killing Joke, we might have rethought our look – in fact, we might not have gone at all.

When we arrived, the band made a beeline for us – well, for Mel actually – and one of them asked her out. He didn't like it when she said no and we felt the tension, coupled with the stress of live TV. We were trying to avoid the band while we were waiting to go on set when the comedian and actor Billy Connolly strode past – he had just been interviewed and looked a bit shell-shocked. He gave each of us a big hug and said kindly, 'Beware of the audience!', then told us how much his wife Pamela

Stephenson loved our clothes. We were so thrilled, we almost skipped into the TV studio.

The presenter had a fashion student with him, who he said would ask us a couple of questions, but she was more nervous than we were and he had to pull the interview back on track. This wasn't helped by the general unease in the audience – mostly Killing Joke fans waiting for them to appear – and they started heckling, which felt intimidating. Billy was right, they were awful. It was a bit much for Mel, who didn't say a word – she was frozen with stage fright – but the rest of us came up with something to say and I managed to keep my cool throughout. It didn't faze me too much; it never has done, being in front of the camera.

Even after a decade we were still regularly surprised by our success. Our name was out there, alongside all the designers who had inspired us to join the industry. We weren't just on the lips of the Camden community, the fashionistas and the rag trade but we were also well regarded amongst the high-profile and famous – actors, musicians, artists, the super-wealthy. We were contacted weekly by managers, stylists and costume designers and we were thrilled to be asked but treated them no differently from all our other customers.

When we started Swanky Modes we wanted to make clothes for people like us who needed an alternative to what high street fashion was offering. We thought about the design, cut and fabric of a garment more than we ever

⊗ Here I am, a happy 4-year-old in Bawtry, wearing a dress which was hand smocked by my mum. I am holding my doll, Charlotte, who I lost and then replaced with another doll … called Charlotte.

⊗ I always loved rummaging in my mum's wardrobe and dressing up in her finery. I do look rather pleased with myself here, bedecked in her clothes and a necklace I had made.

⊗ This is the photo I mentioned on page 22. It is easy to spot me. In a group of happy, smiling faces I am the only serious one!

⊗ My first Holy Communion at school with one of the nuns who taught me. My parents gave me the little prayer book which is dangling from my arm and Aunt Sheila took the photograph.

☺ *Above*: Look at my dad's shiny car! I talk about this picture on page 25. From left to right is Aunt Betty's son, Aunt Betty, me, cheeky Angus, the boy from next door and thoughtful Christopher.

☺ *Left*: The day my dad was awarded an OBE. A proud line-up of Mum, Fiona, me and Dad outside Buckingham Palace. I remember going to a big department store in Bedford, where Mum bought me my coat, which I was very happy with.

⊗ *Left*: 'Dressed as a peacock!' my mum used to say when referring to outfits like this one. I found this children's patchwork dressing gown in a charity shop and wore it as a dress, pairing it with a tartan scarf and straw bag.

⊗ *Below*: This photo sums up the early Swanky Modes years. Me, sat astride my boyfriend's motorbike outside the Camden shop, wearing an all-in-one made from car upholstery.

⊗ *Above*: The legendary Swanky Modes team. Taken by our friend, photographer Janette Beckman, I am bottom-middle, Willie is the blonde on the right, Judy is on the left and Mel is behind me.

⊗ *Left*: The iconic Grace Jones in the Swanky Modes Padlock dress which is now in the Museum of London.

© Willie Christie

⊗ *Left*: An iconic outfit for *Bridget Jones's Diary*. This is just one of many I have made for the film industry over my 50-years-and-counting career.

© *LANDMARK MEDIA / Alamy Stock Photo*

⊗ *Right*: The Swanky Modes Amorphous dress is now in the V&A archive. A little piece of fashion history.

© *Victoria and Albert Museum, London*

⊗ *Left*: Me, wearing a fabulous, crochet inspired, sequinned jacket by the fashion designer Ashish Gupta, who I have worked with for 20 years. The look is reminiscent of one of my earliest transformation projects, when I turned a crochet blanket into a skirt for a big ball I was going to.

© *Sonam Tobgyal*

⊛ On *The Great British Sewing Bee*, encouraging and advising one of the contestants, Farie. I am wearing the necklace I made from sanitiser bottles during the COVID pandemic. © *Love Productions 2021*

⊛ Behind the Seams with Patrick Grant, my friend and partner in judging on *The Great British Sewing Bee.* © *Love Productions 2020, Rosie Geiger*

⊗ In my happy place, pattern cutting. This photograph was taken for the book *Exploding Fashion* and shows what it can take to work on a pattern. Here, I am cutting out a replica of a Vionnet garment. © *Liam Leslie*

⊗ The Three Musketeers – me with my friends and Central Saint Martins colleagues Patrick Lee Yow and Louis Loizou. © *Carlos Duro Yague*

considered its cost and retail value. Money was so low down on our reasons for establishing a fashion house and maybe at least one of us should have been more financially savvy but we weren't. We all shared a powerful work ethic, but none of us were interested in accounts and admin.

Whatever happened in our lives – money worries, depression, relationships, babies, heartbreak, marriage – we had each other, the business, a rack of clothes we loved to wear and regular parties to wear them to. We loved where we were too. We would pop to The Bumble Bee Cafe up the road for our morning wholemeal loaf, affectionately known as the 'hippy house brick' – it was deliciously dense and seedy. For lunch, we often went to the Greek Cypriot café on Camden Road, run by Marxists who left propaganda newspapers out on the tables and there was always a gaggle of old Greek Cypriot men talking animatedly and playing backgammon in a corner. We would order the bean and spinach stew and bring it back on plates to the workshop. That was how we did takeout in those days, on proper crockery.

Most importantly, we formed close bonds with each other's families, relationships that are just as strong today. Swanky Modes was founded and run by three working mothers and one working auntie – me. I never had children or felt the slightest bit broody. If the time and the person had been right, maybe things would have been different but instead I was surrounded by my wonderful nieces and the gorgeous kids of my fashion partners. Willie,

Mel and Judy all say I was the motor of the business, the one constant who could keep going while they broke away to entertain toddlers, pick up children from school, make tea and help with homework. It was good that one of us was there consistently and I never resented this as there was always an equality in what we did. The others worked incredibly hard and were experts at juggling the many demands of family and career – Judy described it as sometimes feeling like she had one foot nailed to the floor. I was in awe of them and have a huge respect for all working mothers.

I think I was a pretty cool 'auntie' when the Swanky Modes offspring were growing up. I'm close to Isla, Mel's daughter, and Tamsin, Willie's daughter. I once took Isla to Mexico and I took Tamsin to the slightly less exotic Margate – I treated her to a stick of rock and some bright plastic hair slides we both had our eye on from a stall on the pier. Willie, Ted, Tamsin and I would spend holidays together in a barn they were renovating in the South of France. We drove over in a van and Tamsin and I would snooze in the back while Willie and Ted took turns to drive. I would often look after Tamsin while the others worked on the barn and I loved hanging out with her – we would go on walks through the village and swim in the local rock pools. I know she has lovely memories of that time too and says we only fell out once when I mistakenly made her porridge in a pan with washing-up liquid in it and couldn't understand why she refused to eat it.

Swanky Modes was a home from home for all the children. When Tamsin was small, we put her in a baby swing seat in the window and she would be entertained by passers-by. When she was older, Willie would pick her up after school and bring her back to the flat above the shop, where the sitting room occasionally doubled up as a fabric cutting room. We would set up a big table and lay out layer upon layer of material and then cut the layers in one go, using a hand-held cutting machine. It was very likely that one of the children would be bathing at this time – the bath was in the kitchen – or watching TV and eating supper together. Tamsin and Ben have memories of a fantastic, laid-back childhood with all the fun and companionship of commune life and an extended 'family' without any of the tricky bits. Other than having to eat Mel's meatloaf, which Mel's son Ben hated and would hide in the pockets of his school trousers!

Ben can remember living in the flat above Swanky Modes like it was yesterday, even though he was only five when they moved in. He says it was never dull and very different from his school friends' more 'normal' lives, which he occasionally wished for. Instead he had an extended family of us, our partners and our friends, who were regular faces and he says now, happily, 'I had four mums and seven dads.' Once the shop was closed, the kitchen would be full of the sounds of chatter and laughter and there was always someone popping in to sit with him and his sister Isla on the sofa so they felt part of things. It's a joy (and a relief) to hear Ben talk about those times now and say how lucky he was to grow up in such an environment where he felt safe and loved. He realises now how young we all were at the time, which may be why it was so much fun for the children.

Tamsin especially loved being part of it all and was always dressing up. There were so many clothes to choose from and no fancy dress outfit was too far-fetched or ambitious in design. There are some hilarious photographs of Isla and Tamsin dolled up in chainmail Lycra swimsuits that they had taken from the shop. One Christmas, Tamsin was given a turquoise and black lace babydoll nightdress with matching dressing gown, which sounds like an inappropriate gift in today's world, but she had been admiring it for weeks in the shop so I made a mini version for her and she was thrilled.

We loved Christmas at Swanky Modes and would make great presents for each other and Christmas stockings to sell in the shop. They were made from transparent plastic with tinsel around the top and Tamsin would help us stuff them with little treats like rain hats, bright nail varnish, small items of jewellery (mostly vintage) and lurex socks.

The shop was a very sociable place. A vivid, bonkers beacon of creativity in the middle of Camden, it attracted other designers, musicians and friends as well as valued customers and those popping in to see what all the fuss was about. When Isla was about six, she made a Guy Fawkes and sat outside the shop collecting money. Tamsin loved sitting in the shop too – she was an excellent shop girl – surrounded by the clothes and enthralled by the visitors. She was very excited when the band Madness started hanging out in the shop. I don't think you have the sort of childhood Tamsin did and then go and do something completely different. She didn't stand a chance! Her career path followed fashion and she now teaches pattern cutting at Central Saint Martins with me.

The productive and supportive family environment between the four of us extended to those who came to work for us. We knew how important it was to inspire and empower the next generation coming into an industry that was changing rapidly. Over the years, we nurtured fantastic young talent – we learnt as much from them as they did from us – and several of our staff went on to build incredible careers in film and fashion. Like Jane Dilworth, one of our first Saturday girls, who was still at school when she came to us and then went on to Central Saint Martins before moving into film editing. And Louise Wilson, who joined us on a work placement and kept us supplied with biscuits. She was incredibly focused when she was with us in the studio and would also have us in fits of laughter with tales of a boyfriend in Paris. Even after she left, she would come back and help us for every collection. She became the course director for the Fashion MA at Central Saint Martins in 1992 until her tragic untimely death in 2014.

Swanky Modes had a reputation for being one of the

coolest places to work and we would involve our assistants in every aspect of the business. We wanted them to know how hard you had to work in fashion to succeed so it was crucial that they experienced every part of the design, make and retail process. This particularly applied to the art college students we took on for six-month work placements. Two of them, the esteemed film costume designers, Rachael Fleming and Steven Noble, became lifelong friends of mine – Steven calls me his 'fairy godmother'.

When I met Steven in the mid-eighties, he was a 16-year-old student from Whitby, a fishing town in North Yorkshire. He was at York Art College and having been chosen by his tutors to work his placement at Swanky Modes, he couldn't have been more thrilled. He'd been following our progress and had seen the *Nova* shoot with the Helmut Newton photographs and was excited by our innovative use of Lycra too. He arrived, fresh off the train, with a head of dreadlocks, a full face of make-up and wearing a pair of voluminous yellow tartan trousers he had made himself. He was going to fit right in instantly, if only we had been there to answer the doorbell when he rang it! While he waited for us, he peered through the windows and fell in love with the place. Steven was a natural and spent his time with us doing everything from running errands, picking up trims and sourcing fabrics to sewing and making up orders. He was also terribly brazen – when he was introduced to David Hockney, he picked up a napkin and said, 'Will you sketch me?' Of course, David was appalled. We missed Steven when his six months were up and he returned to college but we knew that we hadn't seen the last of him.

In the late 1970s I split up with Phil – I felt the relationship had run its course – and moved into the GLC flat that my friends Candy Amsden and Alf were leaving. Some time later, Camden Council took over from the GLC – they had plans to rehouse all the GLC tenants but unfortunately, I wasn't on their list. As the regular tenants moved out, the flats started to be squatted by drug addicts and their dealers. It was a very frightening time – in fact, someone visiting one of the flats was murdered – so I moved out quickly.

I was homeless, staying with different friends, so I applied to the Peabody Estate, a housing association who were at that time housing single creative people. While Swanky Modes had been successful and influential, we hadn't made any money out of it. In 1983, I moved into one of their flats in an area between the Barbican and Old Street. Being housed by the Peabody was a lifesaver and I'm still there today. I have tenure for the rest of my life. The place was just as vibrant with youth and creativity then as it is now.

It was the first time in my life I had lived completely alone and I loved it. There was a great party scene with everyone piling down to The Bricklayer's Arms, but the real place to go was the gay bar, The London Apprentice. I would often be stopped by people asking for directions to it. It was around then that I decided to stop partying quite so hard. I'm genetically programmed to be a workaholic, like my dad and my brother Chris, and the business took most of the hours in my day. To avoid burnout, I went to Greece on holiday – to the small oregano-scented island of Sifnos with my then boyfriend Mervyn – and we walked everywhere, exploring the sandy beaches and whitewashed little houses. I never had any spare cash but always made sure I had enough to live on and to get me to Sifnos every year. Isla often accompanied me as a teenager and still likes to visit the island with me today.

I did make one big purchase: I bought a beach hut on the North Kent coast. I had no intention of leaving London but I would often spend weekends with Anne Martin, who worked with me at Swanky Modes, at her mum's house there. They had a beach hut too and I was obsessed with the idea of owning one. Occasionally an owner would put a postcard on their hut saying 'For Sale' so Anne kept an eye out and waited for one to come up in the front row – I wanted an uninterrupted view of the sea. When it did, I moved swiftly before someone else snapped it up. It coincided with my brother-in-law Peter generously sharing some of his company bonus with me and my siblings so I spent my £500 on a beach hut. This meant I now had a permanent place to escape and could also be near to friends, although you weren't allowed to stay overnight in a beach hut. Later, I bought another hut further along the coast where I could stay the night, but a private company bought the land and knocked my hut down. Luckily, I hadn't yet sold the first one, so I still had my own little piece of heaven, where I could be alone to watch the unbelievable sunsets or invite people over to share bags of hot, salt and vinegary chip suppers.

As well as getting away to the coast, I also liked to travel if I could afford it. My brother Jeremy was now working for Reuters and they had posted him to Mexico. He asked all of the family if they wanted to come and visit, but I was the only one who actually did it. Once I was there, I could stay with him so the main expense was the flight. I went for Christmas in 1985 and stayed in Mexico City, where he lived. It's a huge city, which had a population of about 14 million in those days and quite a lot of pollution. It also has a rich heritage, with ancient pyramids to the north at Teotihuacan and lots of wonderful murals all over the city by Rivera, Orozco, Tamayo and many others. A favourite spot of Jeremy's was the Casa Azul, where Frida Kahlo had lived with Diego Rivera. There were lots of interesting markets for me to browse in as well – heaven!

For Christmas we decided we would fly down to Oaxaca (pronounced 'Wahaca') and had booked a very early flight on 22 December. However, we went out for a meal with Jeremy's flatmate, Luke, the night before and got back very late. We stayed up for a bit, considering whether to just stay up all night and go for the early flight, but felt too exhausted, so decided to have three hours' sleep. We struggled to get up and Luke drove us to the airport, running late, but still in time for the flight. When we got to the check-in desk – chaos! Hundreds of people in a massive crowd, shouting and pushing. Jeremy fought his way to the front and waved the tickets. 'Too late,' they said, 'we've given those seats away. All the flights are fully booked.'

We went out of the terminal feeling rather forlorn. 'There's always a way in Mexico,' pronounced Luke cheerily. He accosted a taxi driver and asked how much a taxi to Oaxaca would cost – a mere 300 miles. It was the only way to get there, and it actually wasn't that expensive, so we got in the cab – a VW Golf – and Luke ostentatiously took down the number and the taxi registration, just in case. We set off, then on the outskirts of the City they pulled over and explained that it was a long way to drive in a VW Golf (and this one was quite battered), they didn't think it would make it all the way so they had arranged for a better car with two friends. We didn't seem to have much choice and it was a much nicer car, so we said okay.

Jeremy seemed quite calm about it all, so I thought it would be fine and anyway, he had got a map out to track progress. Unknown to me, he became alarmed when the driver took a left turn and headed north when he should have taken a right turn and headed south. He still seemed calm, although I was a bit concerned when he surreptitiously got most of his money out of his wallet and hid it in his sock. Later, he told me that when they turned the wrong way, he thought maybe they were going to rob us, perhaps even kill us: *Mum's going to be so pissed off with me if I've got Esme murdered*, he thought. And of course when Luke reported us missing, the taxi driver would just say, 'They didn't like the car so they got out and got in another one.'

No mobile phones in those days.

Jeremy asked if we could stop to get some refreshments somewhere, so we pulled over at a stall by the side of the road. He chatted to the drivers about the route and casually mentioned that he had thought that we would take the road to the south and showed it to the driver. The driver looked a bit uncomfortable and explained that they had just made a diversion to get petrol at a good price and we would be heading that way soon. Jeremy didn't press it – no point making the driver look foolish – but he kept following progress on the map. We did then head south and the driver would ask occasionally which road Jeremy thought he should take. They had just got lost – phew! We arrived in Oaxaca in the late afternoon and Jeremy gave the two drivers a big tip, more out of relief than anything else.

We had a great time in Oaxaca, stayed in a fantastic Hacienda-style hotel and did lots of sightseeing. There were more pyramids and markets and on 23 December there was the Festival of the Radishes! This is a festival where the contestants carve scenes out of, well, radishes, and they are judged and a winner declared each year. Lots of them were Nativity scenes, but one was a model of the solar system and the whole thing was quite surreal.

We had a lovely Christmas and made sure we arrived in good time for the plane back to Mexico City!

I was then joined by Mel's daughter Isla, who had flown out to Mexico alone at the age of nine – very well looked after by the cabin crew on the plane, of course. Jeremy had to go back to work, but Isla and I set off by bus for the Yucatán in the south-west of Mexico. We stayed in a lovely hotel in Merida recommended by Jeremy and Isla was entertained by the doorman reclining in a hammock by the entrance. I wanted to try the famous Mexican chicken dish, Mole Poblano, which is renowned for having chocolate in the sauce, but actually has about 25 different ingredients including three different types of chilli. The guidebook recommended a restaurant so I set out with Isla to find it. I had rather underestimated how far it was, so she was a bit exhausted by the time we got there, but the Mole Poblano was delicious!

From Merida, we went on to Cancún, by the sea, and took a boat trip to the Isla Mujeres. I bought lots of hats in the markets we visited along the way and when we were flying home, we had to wear them one on top of the other because they were too difficult to pack.

Mel was the first to leave Swanky Modes in 1983. She and Clive were now married, there were three children at home and Clive's hugely successful career as a music producer meant he had to travel regularly. They had also bought a house, which was Mel's first proper home – she had had a peripatetic childhood – so the temptation to nest was strong. Mel left and, sometime later, set up a garden design business. It was hard to say goodbye to her professionally but we were the closest of friends so I knew we would continue to see her. We spent a lot of time together socially and have a store of brilliant tales as a consequence. Here is one of them ...

This story belongs in the vault of random yet precious memories: the day I sat on a windowsill with David Bowie. I was at Cynthia Lole's flat on the Great Western Road. I'd met her through Mel and Clive – she was a music co-ordinator and worked across both the music and film industries. We would all go to parties and gigs together and I knew it would be a great night if Cynthia was out too. Her flat was on the Notting Hill Carnival route so she had an open house every year and served cocktails of Cava with crème de cassis or Midori. Anyone was invited and there were often people Cynthia was working with at the time as well as old friends and their children. It was fun, relaxed and the perfect vantage point for watching the floats go by. There would usually be some party hopping with Cynthia as she knew so many people in the area and we would end up at a big bash at the centre of the carnival – the atmosphere was infectious.

In the mid-eighties, Cynthia was working on Julien Temple's musical film *Absolute Beginners*, co-ordinating all the musicians for the soundtrack. It was just before the August Bank Holiday weekend and she was in the studio with David Bowie and his team. David starred in the film alongside Patsy Kensit, Eddie O'Connell, Anita Morris, James Fox and Edward Tudor-Pole; he was recording the title song, produced by Clive at his Westside studios. His manager Coco asked Cynthia what she was up to for the bank holiday and Cynthia explained that she threw a party every year and they were all welcome. Coco thought David might like it as she didn't think he had ever been to the carnival before and said she would be in touch but Cynthia assumed it wouldn't happen. On Monday morning she had a call from David's driver, asking what the parking was like around there.

David arrived with Coco, his son and his driver and they joined the party, mingling comfortably with everyone there. No one made a big deal of his presence, or tried to take photos or monopolise him. He was just hanging out enjoying the vibe with the rest of us, chatting, queuing in the hall for the loo, watching the floats go past and waving to people. Cynthia, usually unflappable, was a nervous host that day, not that any of us could tell but she felt the pressure of a living legend being in her flat. The atmosphere was great with a party both inside the house and outside on the street, everywhere alive with the sounds of noise and laughter.

At one point I went looking for Mel's daughter Isla, who was about nine at the time. She was in the sitting room chatting to David, who was sitting on a windowsill. I went and sat next to him and we watched the carnival and chatted for a while – I remember talking about the

Italian suit he was wearing. I didn't tell him what I did or mention Swanky Modes – I was never any good at hustling for work. We just hung out for a bit. At one point someone walked past on the street and looked up at the window and shouted 'Oh my God!' at the sight of Bowie. I thought for a moment they might pass out with the shock of it all. David gave them a big wave.

As the final float sailed past, David said he wanted to follow it into the heart of the party so his team and a few people joined him and they danced off behind the disappearing parade. As Cynthia says, no future carnival ever lived up to that one.

The end of the eighties was rapidly approaching. Willie, Judy and I were beavering away at Swanky Modes and designing costumes and pieces for commercials and pop videos as well as putting collections together. We had been joined by a new assistant, Rachael Fleming, who we had met through Steven Noble. They had been at York Art College together and Rachael had moved to London to work in a skirt factory on the Edgware Road. The boss was so awful, she described him as beyond redemption and so after a week of torment, she resigned and came to work with us. Coincidentally, Steven was working at Jasper Conran, where Rachael had worked during her college placement. She was an asset to our business and took a similar role to the one Steven had fulfilled –

working in the shop, sewing, general dogsbody, distribution and, as she says, 'making loads of things that were rubbish'. I know we seemed quite old to her at the time, although we were barely 40, and she was surprised by how wild and fun we were – we loved parties, dancing and wearing the craziest outfits that we had made ourselves for specific events.

Designing and making costumes for commercials was becoming a bigger part of what we did and we worked with several stylists, including Annabel Hodin. Annabel had been a model, discovered by *Vogue*'s Anna Wintour, before stepping into a styling role and she worked with all the top photographers as well as film directors like Ridley Scott, who would cross over into commercials. A lovely fan of Swanky Modes, she would regularly ask us to make things. She and I have continued to work together ever since. We have a shared aesthetic, a curiosity about what's next in fashion and a desire to stay one step ahead. Neither of us is fazed by an extremely demanding brief and we have had more than our fair share of them. Making pieces for commercials is a particular type of skill which is as much about considering all the other elements – the location, movement of the actor wearing the piece and camera position, etc. – as it is the finished product. It requires a technical understanding and a different approach to design and making; it is also about spotting the consequence of a particular action, i.e. if water is involved, how will that impact the costume? As stylist and designer, we need to have solved these issues before others realise they could be a problem.

One example is the outfit I had to make for an actor playing a newsreader wearing a suit, Hawaiian shirt and tie. Then with one pull, the entire outfit had to come off to reveal a T-shirt underneath it. It was a special effect without the help of computers. Steven and I had to print the fabric overnight and then I met Annabel at Paddington station and we raced to the studio. Amazingly, the actor did the reveal in one take – I will take a little credit for my construction making this easier!

For the Tia Maria stills advert with the iconic model Iman, we had to replicate the shape of the Tia Maria bottle against the backdrop of a Venetian blind, so we put her in a Swanky Modes style bodycon dress – she looked stunning and it was a very well-received campaign at the time. I also worked with Annabel on a couple of outfits for the New Zealand opera singer Dame Kiri Te Kanawa – a ballgown with a double-length skirt so she could stand on a block and look unfeasibly tall for a specific shot and a Union Jack jacket for The Last Night of the Proms, which she wore on the front cover of *The Radio Times*.

I have loved working with Annabel over the years and I know she trusts me and my ability implicitly. She was once double-booked on a job and had to leave me to work on a hair commercial with the Hollywood actress Gwyneth

Paltrow but said she never worried about what I might say or do because she knew I was the ultimate professional and an expert at problem solving. We often meet up for lunch and she pops in to Central Saint Martins to see what the students are up to and revels in the sustainable direction they are taking. I always make her swimwear too – it's one of my specialist subjects!

In 1989, Willie, one of the cornerstones of Swanky Modes, decided to leave. She had been juggling the pressures of the business and family life for many years and felt it was time for something different so she started teaching at Central Saint Martins. I couldn't imagine Swanky Modes without her but I could see how much she needed a change and that, as with Mel, we would be friends forever. Judy and I continued, with Rachael supporting us, and then Steven returned. By this point Judy had moved to Hastings and was commuting for a couple of days a week so we were thrilled to have Steven back on the team too.

Rachael and Steven both talk about Swanky Modes now with such fondness, I didn't realise then quite how much they loved working with us and the credit they give the business for introducing them to amazing people like directors, photographers and stylists with whom they built working relationships. They both began taking more of a role in the direction Swanky Modes was going and there was a true equality in the way we all worked. I was never very good at being a boss and was much happier in a team environment although Rachael can remember the one and only time I got a bit cross. I had asked her and Steven to paint the hall and staircase in the shop while I was away for the day and left them to choose the paint. Coming back to walls of monstrous pink, I said, 'This is fucking awful, it looks like Elephant and Castle!' – a reference to the shopping centre, which had been painted the weirdest shade.

They repainted it green.

Rachael's illustrious career in costume design started at Swanky Modes. A friend of Judy's was looking for a stylist on a Kim Wilde pop video so Rachael went over with a selection of our dresses. She was nervous because it was her first experience of this type of job and she had been warned that the assistant director was fearsome and screamed at people for no reason. In a state of high anxiety, she came into the dressing room and accidentally swung the plastic bags of clothes against the seeringly hot make-up mirrors. They immediately stuck to the lights and she had to act fast to save the clothes inside. She managed to get through the job without further incident and went on to work on more pop shoots and then a short film, *Butterfly Kiss*, which opened up a new career path in film costume design.

Around the time that Rachael stepped back from Swanky Modes, Judy decided to leave too. The commute was taking its toll and she was establishing a fantastic event space in the old school building she had bought in Hastings. Steven and I produced a collection which we were proud of and was financially successful but the shop lease was coming up for renewal and the industry was evolving. It felt like perfect timing to make a change. We were both doing more costume design, together and individually. Swanky Modes had traversed two revolutionary decades in fashion, with innovation and authenticity. It had consumed me for 20 years and I was happy to let it go. It gave me lifelong friends, the guts to tackle anything, confidence in my creative ability and joy in my heart. How lucky I was to do a job that never felt like work! Something told me if I kept going my luck might run out so we decided to stop and go out on a high. We went out on a party too. Of course we did, you wouldn't expect anything less from the Swanky Modes gang, would you?

I don't remember much about our closing-down party and neither, it seems, does anyone else who was there, so that must mean it was good. Steven said it was 'eventful' and Rachael still has one of the T-shirts we made with the slogan 'RIP Swanky Modes' and the date of its demise. We parked a double-decker bus outside the shop and Rachael's then boyfriend projected the outtakes from the *Arena* documentary and The Alternative Miss World inside like an impromptu cinema. We also put together an exhibition of photographs in the shop, charting our 20-year journey, and I was wearing one of our see-through macs from the final collection – but with other clothes underneath! It was an epic celebration and a surreal and wonderful way to say goodbye.

Recently, the musician Jarvis Cocker, who studied at Central Saint Martins in the 1990s, released a fantasy song called 'Swanky Modes' and it starts with the lines:

There was this shop called Swanky Modes
Just off the top of the Camden Road
You walked past, I recognized you...

It was a fantasy about a girl he had an affair with, who lived in the flat above the shop. It's funny that this came out so recently, a real blast from the past. I don't think any of us really left Swanky Modes and we all have such great affection and pride for it – we never made much money but we were part of fashion history.

CHAPTER 7

Saturday Night At The Movies

One of the jobs I loved at Swanky Modes was working on costume design and making pieces for commercials and pop videos. I was in my element with a quick turnaround and enjoyed the focus of one garment after years of pulling entire collections together. We had also provided outfits for films – like the 'Amorphous' dress that Linda Kozlowski wears in *Crocodile Dundee*, which the costume designer Norma Moriceau sourced from a Sydney store. If someone asked me to get involved in something fun and interesting the likelihood is I would say yes because I was excited by the challenge. Steven felt the same so we decided to find a space we could both work in, on our own projects and for joint collaborations too.

My pal Angela had a jewellery shop called Detail on Endell Street in Covent Garden with a snug basement below the shop, so Steven and I moved there after Swanky Modes closed and created a base for our costume design work. One day, I was cutting a pattern and Steven was sitting at the desk on the phone when we heard a terrible sound: Angela had fallen down the basement steps and bashed her head on the concrete floor at the bottom. The poor woman had had an epileptic fit while serving in the shop. Then running down behind her was the customer, who happened to be the comic and writer Victoria Wood, and she shouted, 'Not to worry, I used to be a medic!' Steven called for an ambulance just in case and Angela was carted off. She was okay, thank goodness, maybe due to Victoria's swift intervention.

It was a tough time financially and work was a bit thin on the ground for a while. By now, you will know that I'm not driven by money, or scared by the lack of it, but I do like to be busy. It felt like a struggle after the Swanky Modes years but I knew, as a freelancer, that this was the nature of the business and I had to hold my nerve. After a couple of years, Angela decided to sell the shop and move to New York to live with her girlfriend so Steven and I moved to a basement underneath an optician on Theobalds Road in Holborn.

The owner called his optician's Gallery Singleton because he had a huge crush on the TV presenter Valerie Singleton and, believe it or not, she even came and opened the shop! Our workshop there was tiny and it was jam-packed full of fabrics and teetering ashtrays – if there had been a fire, we would have been trapped in an inferno of our own making. We dressed it with skeleton fairy lights and Day of the Dead inspired decorations, which I had picked up on my trip to Mexico. Steven added more strings of lights so it felt like a sparkly grotto. There was a space for us both to work and a little chamber which would have been the original Victorian safe room and was stacked, from floor to ceiling, with vintage spectacles. Every so often we would rummage in there if we needed glasses for a commercial. Rachael's assistant at the time, Natalie Ward, would pop in to see us and remembers coming down in the middle of a business meeting Steven was having with clients. There were eight Japanese people and their translator squeezed around my pattern cutting table and she couldn't imagine these smart professionals ever having been to a studio like it – they must have left in a state of shock.

By now, Rachael was also a highly respected costume designer so the three of us would occasionally team up or she would ask one of us to work with her on a project. I'd been so lucky to have the camaraderie of three women throughout the Swanky Modes years that I didn't expect to find it again professionally, yet here I was with two protégés who were becoming titans and taking me along for the ride – I loved the tables turning.

When Steven got the job for a promo for soul singer Luther Vandross, we jumped at it although we had very little time. That was often the way. They gave us 24 hours to make dresses for Luther's backing singers so we were sent basic measurements and expected to arrive in the studio with them the following day. There was no opportunity for a fitting. We sourced a Lycra rubber fabric, cut the patterns and put them together, working through the night, and then Steven took them to the recording studio first thing in the morning and I went home to get some sleep. The next thing I knew, the phone was ringing and I struggled out of bed to pick it up, only to hear Steven panicking on the other end: the dresses didn't fit! The scant measurements had missed vital information and now he was at the studio with the singers in their underwear. I jumped in a cab and dashed to the workshop to pick up my sewing machine and extra fabric and then he and I set up a sewing space where we cut, altered, cursed and remade the dresses. All was well in the end. This was a normal occurrence and I have grown so used to the last-minute panics and curveballs that I tend to expect them now – I no longer hyperventilate!

The optician's love for Valerie Singleton must have been short-lived as he ended up selling the business and turning us out on the streets. Okay, well, it wasn't quite like that, we were ready to leave and we were desperate for more space too. We found the ideal place in Dalston, which, back then, was one of those areas in London that nobody went to unless they lived there. Steven and I loved it. It was much more affordable than Central London and it meant we could sign up for a bigger workshop and have space for two more, so Natalie Ward and Liza Bracey joined us. Natalie had started her career in wardrobe for ITV's *The Bill* before Rachael tempted her over to the world of film – it didn't take much tempting. They continued to work together for many years, often with me and Steven too. Natalie said that when she first met me, she thought I was incredibly cool with an air of mystery about me and the capacity to be a little wild. The thought of that makes me chuckle!

Rachael was now a hugely respected film costume designer and she employed me on many of her productions. She asked me to make Dale Winton's suit for *Trainspotting* and she even had a tiny onscreen part, playing his gameshow hostess, wearing a Swanky Modes 'Flasher' dress from our final collection. I made a cheesecloth shirt for Leonardo DiCaprio in *The Beach* (2000), a ballgown for *28 Days Later...* (2002) and a 'fur' coat for Scarlett Johansson in *Under the Skin* (2013). For *Bridget Jones's Diary* (2001), I made Honor Blackman's pink silk blouse and the infamous bunny outfit Renée Zellweger wears in the party scene – she kept telling me to make it tighter (she wanted to look bigger than she was for the character) and by the end, she couldn't sit down in it. I met her again, years later, for costume fittings for pickups on *Bridget Jones's Baby* (2016). Steven was working on the film but had to move on to the next project, so Natalie came in at the end and we went to Renée's hotel room. As it happened, *The Great British Sewing* Bee was on TV that night and Natalie told Renée about it and she said she would watch it. She told Natalie the following day that she had loved it. Such a sweet thing for her to do.

For the 1996 film *Saint-Ex*, I made a couple of key outfits for Miranda Richardson, including a dress she wore for a party scene. I was also at that party, as an extra. Rachael knew I had a mariachi costume – a traditional Mexican band outfit – which my brother Jeremy had brought back from Mexico for me some years previously. I was invited to come and show it off in the back of shot!

Jeremy now lived in Brussels and was planning a trip back to Mexico with his partner, now wife, Kate. But his cat Wolfgang was sick, so he asked me if I could come over and catsit. I went over with my partner, Mervyn, and settled in. Sadly, Wolfgang took a turn for the worse and died while Jeremy was away. My brother was quite upset, but also mortified that he had lumbered me with dealing with the cat dying.

The cat was in the fridge – at the vet, not at home – and when Jeremy got back, he collected the body because he wanted to bury him himself, not have the vet dispose of him. However, he didn't have a garden.

Where to bury the cat?

Brussels has a lovely forest to the south that Jeremy and Kate would cycle round, so he decided that we should bury the cat there, so they could visit the spot when they were out cycling. He didn't know if that was allowed or not, so decided that the best thing was not to ask, then if someone challenged him he could plead ignorance. A wine box was used for a coffin and we set off for the forest.

There was Jeremy and Mervyn, each with a spade, Kate and me acting as lookout and Wolfgang in the mini coffin. Jeremy selected a spot about 50 yards from the cycle path and he and Mervyn started digging. If Kate or I saw someone on the path or in the forest, we would alert them, they would drop the spades and we would all stand there, admiring the trees and trying not to look too guilty or suspicious.

There was an added complication too. The big news in Brussels in 1996 was about Marc Dutroux, a serial killer who had abducted young girls and murdered them and had then escaped from the police so it was the perfect time to be seen burying a small coffin in the woods …

In my film work I was usually asked to make pieces for the lead characters. Designing and making garments for film was a natural step on from the music and TV gigs I had been doing and gave a fascinating insight into the glamorous world of movie stars and big budgets. I have always loved working as part of a team and this was an uber version of it. Everyone has an input, not just the costume department but the actor and director too and other people you didn't know existed but turn out to be terribly important. There's a lot riding on one little outfit but costume is an integral, vital part of the film. It has to tell the story, it needs to be historically referenced, appropriate for the character, fit for purpose and it must work on screen too. What may look good in the sewing studio may not work in front of the camera or be worth the time and effort it takes.

In the 2007 film *1408*, I had to make a Hawaiian shirt for the American actor John Cusack but because of the storyline I actually had to make ten identical shirts, which meant matching the fabric exactly every time – no mean feat when you're dealing with something so highly patterned. Natalie was the costume designer on the project and she sourced the material in New York. It drove me a little crazy by the end. I also made all the men's shirts for *Captain Corelli's Mandolin* (2001). The production team asked me if I would hand sew the buttonholes too and I said, 'Yes, if you've got a couple of months.' They hadn't so I didn't do it. There are certain things that aren't worth it and won't be noticed on screen.

I cut every pattern for Steven and he described me as his 'right arm'. It was such a fun time – I was working with two of my closest friends doing the job I loved. We have our share of funny anecdotes but people are often disappointed by my answer to their question, 'Who is the worst famous person you have worked with?' The truth is nobody has ever been really rude or mean to me. I have never had a bad experience or felt intimidated. That might sound impossible to believe but it's true and when I talked to Rachael recently about this she laughed. She said she thinks celebrities wouldn't dream of being unkind to me because I wouldn't stand for it. Or I probably wouldn't notice. I have never been bothered by what other people think or how they may behave towards me and it's kept me sane in a crazy industry. I treat everyone the same and approach each new thing with a good level of enthusiasm and energy but if something goes wrong, well then, that's life! I could say this philosophy comes with age but I know it's been with me from early on so perhaps it comes with being sent to boarding school at the age of five?

The only time I was a little star-struck was when I met Hollywood movie star, Dustin Hoffman. He came into our studio for a costume fitting for his next film, *Last Chance Harvey* (2008), which I was helping Natalie with. I tried to maintain a cool, professional composure but I was in awe of him. Natalie invited me to the wrap party so I shimmied along, hair teased into a beehive and imagine my surprise when Dustin insisted on dancing with me. He grabbed my hands and spun me round, almost off my feet. The two of us were a frenzy of music and energy and I think we must have cleared the dance floor with our crazy moves. My beehive was not the same after that experience!

I have worked on more films than I can count or remember but there are some jobs that stick in my mind[2], like the 2014 film *The Two Faces of January* with Viggo Mortensen and Kirsten Dunst. Steven was the costume designer on it and I was cutting the patterns and made most of Kirsten's outfits. We had set up our studio ready for Kirsten to arrive for her fittings but had a message at the last minute to say she couldn't make it over and could we fly to LA instead? Of course we could, so we packed up our studio, went straight to the airport and were excited (okay, overexcited!) to discover we had first-class

---

2 Turn to page 275 for a full list of the films I have worked on.

flights. As an aside to this story, the week before I had been talking to an American student (who was working with me) about travel and said I had only been in first class once, which was a trip to Brussels with my mum and brother, where we were upgraded. The difference between first and standard class on that flight was a curtain and a glass of champagne so I didn't feel it really counted.

Imagine my surprise when just a week later, I had a first-class ticket to LA and found myself lazing around the VIP lounge before we boarded. We took full advantage of the massages and the Bloody Marys until someone came up to us and said our flight was about to leave, they were shutting the gate. We ran like the wind. Or at least Steven did; he was miles ahead of me with a plan to delay the plane while I struggled to catch up. I think he thought it would be as easy as putting a foot in the door but he had to beg them to wait for me as they ushered him on to the plane. I arrived just in time, sweating profusely, gasping for breath and laughing with the relief of not missing the flight – my one chance at a first-class experience might have been scuppered!

When we arrived, it was late in the evening so we set the hotel room up with the mood boards, sewing equipment and costumes ready for the early-morning fitting and fell into bed. We woke to a message from Kirsten's agent to say she couldn't make it to the hotel but could we go to her parents' house instead so we packed everything up again and headed out. When we got there, she was terribly apologetic, slightly hungover and an absolute angel. That was a fantastic and fun job to work on.

Natalie, Liza, Steven and I moved out of the Dalston workshop because it was being converted into flats and we found a space in London Fields. Steven was away a lot but we had outgrown our old place. I needed more room for my Swanky Modes archive, industrial sewing machines and pattern cutting tables, and Natalie and Liza had amassed an incredible wardrobe of costume over the years. We found somewhere within ten minutes of where we all lived – I could cycle there. It was a studio in an old 1970s GLC building, separated into units, which appealed to me and it was full of artists, some of whom have moved on, but we are still there, along with a vibrant mix of designers and makers.

Freelance life suited me very well but occasionally I panicked about my workload. Like the time I worked with Cher. In 1998, she was over in the UK, recording an album for Rob Dickins at Warner Brothers. Cynthia introduced us as she was looking for someone to do dress alterations. She gave me an exquisite, very expensive YSL sequinned jacket that needed to be altered. What I didn't know was the sequins were hand sewn and knotted off individually as opposed to the mass-produced version I was used to, where they just unravel. I had to unpick the sides, take the sequins off and then sew them back on, one by one.

I would go and see Cher in the mews house she was renting off Oxford Street and she was great to work with.

When her PR people phoned me a year later to ask if I would take on more work for her, I'm not sure why I said no. At the time I was very busy and I think I made an excuse about not being able to prioritise her but I think I was scared about being consumed by Cher, with no time to do anything else. I should have said yes and worked it out as I went along; I wish I had. Not because it would have changed my life – I didn't want it changing – but because it would have been an amazing experience.

What links these experiences, people and garments are my scissors and my sewing machine. I never feel out of my depth if I'm doing the thing I love and know that I'm good at. When Juliette Binoche was cast as a seamstress in Anthony Minghella's 2006 film *Breaking and Entering*, Natalie, who was the costume designer on the production, asked if I would meet Juliette so she could understand more about the role she was playing. She was keen to watch me work so she came to my studio and sat quietly in the corner as I measured, cut and sewed. I forgot fairly quickly that Juliette, the movie star, was there and afterwards she said one of the most important things she had learnt was how sewing sent me into my own little world. She's right. It's one of the most wonderful things about creating something – as you work, you can think about stuff, consider problems or be distracted from them. It is often a meditative process and people regularly tell me how much sewing has helped them through low periods of their life.

Which leads me on to the death of my dad in 1992. He had been diagnosed, too late, with prostate cancer swiftly followed by dementia so things were not looking good. He was still living at home with Mum and we all took it in turns to visit every week. Even in the midst of his dementia, he was utterly charming and thoughtful. I remember sitting with him watching TV and there was a shot of a beautiful beach, with a turquoise sea and huge leafy palm trees. He stood up, held his hand out to me and said, 'Come on, let's go there.'

When Mum needed a break, Dad would go to a respite centre. He would regale them with his intrepid war stories, which they assumed must be complete fantasy because of the dementia, but when Mum collected him, they asked her and she said it was all true. Although, when I went to see him there another time, he introduced me to one of the other patients as his helicopter pilot. Luckily for him, I think, and for us too, he died of cancer before the dementia destroyed him. We helped Mum care for him at home until the end when the amazing Macmillan nurses came to help and we were all there when he died, aged 72.

At his funeral the Royal Air Force sent two senior officers to pay their respects, as they probably usually do, but Dad's driver from the seventies also came, as well as an old chap who had been in the hospital with him during the war. I chatted to him and he said when he saw that Dad had died, he had to come to the funeral because my dad had kept everyone's spirits up when they were recuperating in the hospital – that was the kind of man he was.

I found it so hard to believe he had gone even though it happened in front of me. He had been such an adored life force in our family, I wasn't sure how we would all cope but our main concern was for Mum.

CHAPTER 8

Central Saint Martins

After Dad died, I grew closer to Mum and my siblings and I visited her weekly – she was always at the centre of our family gatherings. She was unchanged in many ways but also somehow softer, more accepting and less quick to judge me. Her sense of humour and ridiculous snobbery were both still firmly in place and she made me laugh often, although she didn't always mean to. Like revelling in the fact that my brother-in-law was a member of the Royal Yacht Squadron and was allowed to fly the white ensign from his sailing boat, a flag used only by the royal family and the squadron. We all loved going on his boat, it was great fun and we would go to watch the annual cricket match on the Brambles sandbank in the Solent, which would briefly appear above water at low tide.

My brother Chris is very generous to his family – whenever we went on holiday together he would pay for me and once bought me a washing machine when I couldn't afford one. One year, Chris and I went to France on holiday with our parents and loved eating out. On one particular occasion we headed to a local restaurant but within a few minutes of arriving, we realised something was up when the waiter came to our table and behaved in a belligerent manner. He was drunk and impatient with our dithering over the menu. He took our order and then one of us decided to change our mind. There was a pause, we held our collective breath and then the waiter tore up our order in a theatrical and rather threatening manner. Then we changed our order for a second time and he ripped the order to shreds, again! We did manage to get fed in the end but the entire experience was pretty miserable and we were glad to get out of there. When we came out we sat on a bench in the village square to give us a chance to recover from the ordeal.

But Mum intuitively saw the funny side of it and recounted the story in such an amusing way that she completely changed our mood and had us all laughing out loud. In that moment I recognised in her a special talent for seeing things from a different point of view; a talent that she had always had, but that really crystallised for me that evening. I don't think that I know anyone else who could have managed to turn things around in that way, transforming a very forgettable experience into a treasured memory.

I think Mum had been ill for a while but she covered it up, from us and possibly from herself, for some time. We were all at a family party in 1999 and I remember looking across and seeing Mum sitting on a bench and being surprised by that. She loved a social event and was usually the life and soul of them so it was strange to see her sitting down. Maybe she was just feeling a little below par. Quite soon after, Chris went around to see her. She loved cooking and always insisted on making us supper but this time she didn't offer to cook. In fact, she was too tired to go out and buy food but she didn't tell Chris that at the time.

Whether she decided to go to the doctor or we pushed her into it, I can't remember, but she was referred to the hospital for a scan later the same year. I was with her when she collected her results from her GP – she was diagnosed with lung cancer, which had then spread. She said afterwards that she wished she had been alone because she wouldn't have told anyone and just got on with it. That was typical of my mum and the stiff upper lip generation she belonged to. Ironically, some years earlier when talking about the growing evidence of the damage to health caused by cigarettes, she said, 'I've smoked all my life and they've never done me any harm.' Well, they had now. We went back to her house and then my brother Chris came over to be with her as I had to go to the workshop. I planned to stop off at the petrol station on my way as I had run out of tobacco for my roll-ups, but as I cycled past, I just kept going – I had smoked for about 35 years and in that moment I decided to stop and haven't touched a cigarette since.

⊗ ⊗ ⊗

As we had done with Dad, we looked after Mum at home on a rota of visits, sitting with her, holding her hand and sharing memories. She and I had grown much closer in recent years and I valued the time I had with her and the new understandings we had forged. I took extended leave from work and spent a lot of time there. I remember one day we discovered a wasp nest in the extension and a chap came in to get rid of it. Mum was in bed and I was in her room, standing at the window, absent-mindedly watching the man put up a long ladder against the side of the house. He began to climb the rungs and as he got almost to the top, the ladder suddenly swayed and fell sideways with him on it. It was like watching him in slow motion and I gasped and ran out to the garden. Luckily for him, he had landed on the lawn and missed the raised brick flower beds so he was fine, just a bit shaken.

When the nurses told us Mum was close to the end, we called the priest in to perform the Last Rites. As a Catholic, albeit a non-practising one, we thought it would have been what she wanted or expected. We were all there on our knees around the bed when the priest dropped the stopper from the Holy oil bottle he was holding, in between the folds of Mum's nightie, so he had to scrabble around to get it back. Poor man! I put my forehead on the bed and afterwards my siblings said they thought I was sobbing. In fact, I was biting the bedclothes to stop myself having a fit of the giggles from the tension and comedy of the situation.

When Mum died, I was the only one in the room. Everyone else had gone downstairs for a cup of tea and I was sitting with her for a while. I got up and said I was going to pop down for a cup of tea too but I wouldn't be long. At the door I paused and then turned back to look at her. A moment later, she died. I wonder if she thought I had already left the room and so she could let go – she was a very private person and I don't think she would have wanted an audience for her final moments.

After Mum died, I was sitting in the kitchen of her house with my brother Jeremy. We thought we should let her GP surgery know that she had passed away, so I called them. Jeremy was listening to my side of the conversation, but he quickly worked out what was going on.

'I'm calling about Mrs Young …'

'Christian names? Patricia Josephine.'

'Address is Earl Road.'

'Date of birth was 19 March 1921.'

Of course they have to go through all of the questions to identify who they are dealing with, but Jeremy could see what was coming and started giggling – more nervous tension.

'Her doctor is Doctor John.'

'I'm her daughter.'

Jeremy had now found a napkin and was biting it so that he didn't start laughing in the background. Then finally …

'She's dead.'

Jeremy had to leave the room at this point and afterwards we were both in mild hysterics.

I didn't expect Mum's death to affect me the way it did. She had been ill for a while and I had been with her throughout her decline so I assumed I must have done a lot of my grieving already. Instead I was thrown by how upset I was. After Dad's death I had focused on her and now they were both gone, I felt lost without them. It was like I was adrift, not attached to the earth. I didn't go off the rails, have counselling or hide, I just focused on my work and kept moving forward as the feeling began to dissipate. It took a couple of years for me to come to terms with the death of them both.

When I sorted through Mum's things I found a card I had painted for her when I was about three and already fascinated by art. It surprised me because Mum wasn't sentimental but she had kept it all these years and now it's a valued possession of mine.

It's funny how some things come full circle, isn't it? My little card found its way back to me and then quite soon after, I found myself back at my old art school, Central Saint Martins. I was focused on my film costume design career and generally happy with my lot when I had a call in 2000 from a past Swanky Modes assistant, Louise Wilson. Louise, after years of working with fashion designers, was now professor of fashion and head of the MA course at Central Saint Martins and she wanted to talk to me about one of her students, Ashish Gupta.

Ashish was doing an MA in fashion at Central Saint Martins and was working with Louise on his final collection. He was initially inspired by the character of Dorothy in *The Wizard of Oz* but had grown the idea into metal-boned, corseted tweed evening dresses with giant bows that pierced through the fabric. They were a feat of engineering. Louise looked at the sketches, talked to Willie Walters – the course director for the Fashion BA – and then they told him there was only one person who could help – me. Ashish was the first student I taught at CSM and we both worked hard on realising his designs. He remembers coming to the little studio I had at the time in Holborn. It was the evening and I was making a dress from the collection (it was easier for me to tackle it because I understood the construction) and he was very grateful and a little shocked that I was working so late for him. He always says he couldn't have done the collection without me. I'm sure he could have done but we both enjoyed the collaboration and this set the tone for our future relationship.

Willie asked me to stay on and teach pattern cutting with BA Fashion Print students, which really appealed to me so I accepted a part-time position. I turned up on my bicycle, hair piled on top of my head, and being back was surreal – it was like I'd never been away in many respects but, of course, so much had changed in the years that had passed. Willie was such an inspiration to me and I was delighted to be working with her again. She loved her job and was hugely supportive and protective of her staff, encouraging them to spend as much time as possible with their students rather than sitting at a computer drowning in paperwork.

One of the reasons I was keen to take the job, other than working with pals, was the opportunity to give something back after years of being in the fashion industry. I have always championed the next generation so to take a key role at the beginning of their careers was important to me. It's not that I think I was lucky – we worked ridiculously hard to build and maintain Swanky Modes – but it was a different time and if I could use my knowledge to help others realise their dreams then I should. I have always been passionate about finding ways to promote the young, underprivileged and minority groups and make sure everyone has access to opportunities. I continue to voice this and am active in helping where I can.

My role was as senior lecturer on the BA Print course. Occasionally the offer of a full-time role came up, but I resisted as I wanted to be open to other things, so I work part-time, teaching pattern cutting and running a swim-wear and lingerie course from a workshop space on the fashion floor. I used to share the job with the fabulous Patrick Lee Yow, who, unlike me, was trained in classic pattern cutting techniques. He can remember when he first met me. He was replacing someone I had worked with so he came up to my floor and saw a woman with red lipstick, a short bob and glasses, who looked him up and down and pursed her lips. He knew I was sizing him up! To begin with, he wouldn't engage with me and I found it hard so I kept asking people what I should do about it. Some people advised that I should confront him, but my brother Chris said, 'Why don't you just invite him out for a drink?' The first time he said no, but the next time we went for a coffee and we formed a really strong connection. That was over 20 years ago and colleagues describe us as something of a dynamic duo. We don't teach together anymore, but our workspaces are next to each other so we can still chat and compare notes.

Patrick and I love throwing ourselves into the creative maelstrom of our students' originality, working well beyond our allotted hours and celebrating hard-won results. Our shared background in design gives us a real understanding of where the students are heading and we thrive on their determination and achievements as much as they do. When we worked more closely together, it gave the students the benefit of two very different approaches and in turn, they would often surprise us with their work. The key to our success has been the trust we hold in each other and the total lack of our own egos. It is all about the students producing the very best work they can, not who is the best tutor. The fashion courses are unique – I don't know of another school that teaches as we do and focuses on the student and their vision rather than leading with technical ability.

Along with senior lecturer Louis Loizou, Patrick and I are dubbed 'The Three Musketeers' and Louis often refers to our threesome as The Good (Louis), The Bad (Patrick) and The Ugly (me!). I refer to it differently – I'm the good and Louis is the ugly! Louis says he was a little scared of me when we first met and still finds my exacting stare disconcerting, particularly when I spot him using a studio space with his students that I was hoping to nab. Before he was a tutor, he would often catch the number 29 bus down to Gordon Square, which took him past Swanky Modes. He used to marvel at the colour and vibrancy of the shop, so he was surprised and thrilled to be working with two of the founding members. Louis also remembers when we were moving from Charing Cross to the new space and there was an undercurrent of dissent about leaving the hallowed building. Students had staged a protest by putting up angry posters with yellow duct tape and I was spotted admiring the handiwork so rumour got around that it was me! It wasn't, but I do love a bit of anarchy.

It was in 1989 that St Martin's merged with the Central School for Art and Design and in 2011, we left the old Charing Cross Road building I loved as a student and moved to Granary Square in King's Cross. It's a striking, architecturally designed conversion of a 19th-century granary building, with lots of concrete, glass and wood set around a central atrium, and it now houses courses from Fashion, Photography and Art to Ceramics, Architecture and Film. The place pulsates with creativity, skill and talent, which is infectious for both students and teachers alike. Everywhere is open plan so you can walk from one course to the next and instantly know which section you are in by either the garments on the mannequins, the screen print paint splashed across the floors, the pattern blocks and the rolls of fabric. You can also tell what stage students are at in the process and whether they are building up for a 'crit', where they show us and their peers their work. Those days beforehand are filled with tense, focused energy and the lecturers are buzzing around the making studios, giving advice and support. This is a big moment for everyone after weeks of working on a project and I'm often in awe of what is produced.

Central Saint Martins has always attracted some of the very best lecturers – those I learnt from many years ago and those I have taught alongside in the last couple of decades. They have been hugely important people in my teaching career and I'm grateful to have had them as colleagues and friends. We all share the same beliefs, namely that the tutor is not the font of all knowledge. We love it if a student proves us wrong! There are things we don't know and mistakes that we may make but we take the journey with our students and encourage them to question themselves and us. Some embrace this and blossom, others feel insecure because they want clear explanations, rights and wrongs and definitive answers, but fashion design isn't like that. The magic comes from the grey areas of boundary pushing and experiment, of knowing the basics and then subverting them.

With those students that struggle with the lack of structure and surety, we work at building their confidence and encouraging them to take risks. Sometimes when I give feedback and guidance I am told to bugger off and occasionally the student is right to say that but I want them to demonstrate why they are. I always encourage them to experiment and if they get it wrong, then build better work from it. It's so satisfying when a student finds their way, whether in fashion or in the realisation that fashion is not the direction they want to head and they take a diversion into other creative areas such as the art world or the music industry. We help them step beyond the conventional routes to achieve their vision, and seeing how they all develop and grow over the four years of the course is wonderful.

I like to get to know the students and understand their motivations and also help them bond as a group and learn from each other, the way I have learnt from my many collaborators all my life, so some socialising is also on the agenda – who would have thought? Sometimes I arrange an outing for them to my beach hut and I prepare a big picnic and we hang out and go swimming.

Although I'm not too fussed about age and birthdays, you will have gathered by now that I do like a party! I had lots for my 60th birthday and I wanted the beach hut to be part of it, so I decided to have lots of friends and family down for a party by the seaside in the summer of 2009. During the day we would all hang out at the beach hut and then have an evening do – I just had to find a good venue. I tried various places near the hut – the two local sailing clubs, the hall in the high street, but they were either booked or unsuitable. Finally, Anne Martin and her sister Alanah said I should have it at the house that they had inherited from their mum. Lots of the guests were musicians, so there were some performances – by Bette Bright (Anne), Clive Langer, Scarlet & Viva, and also by my niece Alice, who was in a band with her then partner Finn, and Caroline, another niece, was compère.

Caroline observed to Anne and Alanah that it was very nice of them to host the party and Alanah replied, 'We wouldn't do this for just anyone – we love your auntie.'

I've been so lucky to have such good friends, and sadly Alanah died a few years later, having contracted the awful and incurable disease pancreatic cancer. I will always miss her.

My brother Jeremy and his wife Kate had helped in setting up my 60th party and decided they liked the area and would go house hunting down there. They don't have a car, so took their bikes on the train, then cycled to see the houses. Late in the afternoon I got a call from Jeremy: Kate had had an accident and had fractured her skull and been taken to hospital in an air ambulance. I found out where the hospital was and said I would see him there. It was in Essex, so I wasn't sure how I would get there, but Mel's daughter Isla came to the rescue. I called her up and without hesitation she dropped what she was doing and drove me there. Jeremy was understandably very distressed and was going to stay the night nearby so Isla drove him back to his house in London to pick up things for Kate and for his stay, then drove him back again. I stayed the night with Jeremy to make sure he was all right – when your family need you, you just have to be there. Kate can't remember anything of the two weeks following her accident, although she kept telling the doctors that she had to go home because she was going to see Madness the next weekend! Happily, she recovered fully.

My siblings wanted to club together to get me something special for my 60th and were keen to have some clue as to what I might like. I was musing over the idea of asking for a ruby ring, although admittedly rubies are more associated with 40th anniversaries. Over dinner at our favourite kebab place, I discussed it with my brother Christopher. He said, 'Well, we can give you a thing or we can give you an experience: how about we pay for a trip to Iran?' He'd accompany me – paying his own way, of course. It was a place he'd wanted to go to for a while and so there was an element of self-interest there, but he thought that it might appeal to me as well and he was right. I immediately saw the attraction: it would be an adventure, somewhere very different to anywhere I had been before and an experience that I would always remember. So yes, Iran it would be.

But what to pack? The perennial holiday question – and particularly important to someone like myself who is interested in clothes and how they are made. They would need to be suitable for the potentially hot climate (or would it be cold in April?), but above all, I wanted to respect Iranian sensibilities and not stick out like a sore thumb in something inappropriate. I decided that the solution would be to make some clothes especially for this trip. I would enjoy doing it and my wardrobe would be 'tailor made' for Iran. So I had some fun making all of my outfits, including a coat, trousers, three dresses and a couple of head scarves. I used linen to be cool and darker colours so as not to be unduly ostentatious. I made everything loose-fitting so as to be comfortable and not too figure-hugging.

I still wear my 'Iranian' outfits to this day.

We set off from Stansted Airport on 31 March 2009 with a sense of anticipation, not at all sure what to expect, but that was all part of the excitement. As the plane descended for landing at Tehran's Imam Khomeini International Airport, all female passengers were asked to put on a headscarf to conform with Iranian require-ments. We exited the plane in the darkness at 4am on 1 April. It was April Fool's Day and we didn't even have a hotel booked.

Was this all such a good idea?

The first hurdle would be the Iranian immigration control. Chris had been to Israel and was concerned that the Israeli stamp in his passport might lead to him being refused entry. And by chance the Iranian visa had ended up right next to the Israeli stamp in his passport and so could hardly be missed. He'd visited the Iranian Embassy in London twice to point out that he had the Israeli stamp and to check whether that would be an obstacle to entry and both times he'd been reassured that there was nothing to worry about. But you never know – immigration officers can wield a lot of power. Now it was crunch time. Well, the immigration officer didn't bat an eyelid and we were nodded through. The Israeli stamp was of no interest and the rumours about it being a problem were unfounded.

We were in Iran and the adventure had begun.

I'd thought that the main places of interest in Iran would be outside Tehran, but the capital exceeded my expectations. We arrived towards the end of the Nowruz holiday – the Iranian new year – and so Tehran was initially quiet, with shops and businesses closed. But there was still plenty to explore.

Getting to grips with the layout of the city, we walked miles and travelled on the Metro from the Darband hills in the north to the Ayatollah Khomeini Mausoleum in the south, taking in palaces, museums, bazaars and ordinary neighbourhoods in between. One museum that particularly stays with me was the Treasury of National Jewels – if you want rubies, boy, have they got rubies! There were plates piled high with sparkling gems, reminding me a bit of the displays of sweets that you used to see in Woolworths, but worth rather more per ounce.

Early on in our stay in Tehran we were in a square, unsuccessfully trying to flag down a taxi, when to our surprise a car stopped with two women inside and they asked us if we would like a lift – they had seen that we were a bit stuck and came to our rescue. They spoke good English and when they found out that we were from London, they asked if we would like to join them and their family in their Nowruz celebrations. Yes please, we certainly would! We went back to their home where we had a meal with their extended family and then accompanied them to a river, where they floated off bits of grass according to tradition. They were wonderfully welcoming and hospitable in a way that would be hard to imagine happening in London.

As we were to discover, this Iranian welcome was not a one-off. When we visited the Khomeini Mausoleum, we were also invited home by a couple for tea and refreshments. These people seemed rather more religiously inclined than the Nowruz family, but equally hospitable. In fact, wherever we went in Iran we found that people were friendly and helpful and genuinely pleased to welcome visiting foreigners.

Naturally enough, I noticed what the women were wearing. In more rural areas and in parts of Tehran the clothing was plain, often black and all-enveloping. Actually, these clothes reminded me very much of what the nuns at my convent used to wear and prompted the thought that the historical origin of the nun's habit is probably shared with this conservative Islamic style. In the north of Tehran, which seemed to be rather well-to-do, the young ladies conformed to the basic dress conventions but used more interesting fabrics and headscarves would be worn almost falling off the back of the head. While not figure-hugging, their clothes would be more shaped and there would be little flourishes of style and individuality. Again, this took me back to the convent and reminded me of how we as schoolgirls had bent the rules on the school uniform to express a little of ourselves.

In the three weeks that we were there, we travelled fairly widely and without any restrictions from the authorities. Chris had done some research so we knew where we wanted to go, but we travelled without a fixed schedule, hopping on and off buses between towns as the mood took us and finding hotels as we went. It just so happened that campaigning was in full swing as President Mahmoud Ahmadinejad sought re-election and rallies occurred in some of the places that we visited, although this didn't have any impact on us.

I found my time in Iran fascinating, but if I had to choose highlights they would have to include the ancient ruins of Persepolis – a UNESCO World Heritage Site – and the possibly even more ancient city of Isfahan.

Cyrus the Great chose the site for Persepolis 2,500 years ago, but it was built by his successor, Darius the Great, and subsequently ruled over by Darius' son, Xerxes the Great. Sadly, it was destroyed in 330BCE by another 'Great' Alexander. These are almost mythical names that come together in this one extraordinary place.

Isfahan's origins may date back even further, possibly as much as 4,000 years, but unlike the ruined Persepolis, Alexander didn't take against Isfahan and it remains a thriving city with impressive architecture including beautiful palaces, bridges and mosques. The Iranian culture and heritage are truly ancient, varied and rich and the Iranians are justifiably proud of it.

Chris' idea of a visit to Iran really was an excellent suggestion and a thought that would otherwise never have crossed my mind. It turned out to be a much better birthday present than a ruby ring, lovely as that might have been. En route, I had many new experiences, including getting caught in a sandstorm in a town in the desert, visiting a Zoroastrian cemetery in the adobe city of Yazd and even receiving my first proposal of marriage from a rather charming stranger in a garden in Shiraz! I've been to many hospitable places around the world, but looking back, I'd have to say that Iran is the friendliest country that I have ever visited, bar none.

⊗ ⊗ ⊗

Back in the world of Central Saint Martins in the early 2000s, it was decided that everyone teaching should have passed a Diploma of Education (DipEd), and even though the pattern cutting that I teach is a very practical and hands-on activity, it applied to me too. That meant a part-time, year-long course – studying, and writing essays, although thankfully not an exam. Even so, essays aren't really my thing – I'm hopeless at typing, my spelling is poor due to my deafness as a child and my handwriting isn't great either. I was bit daunted.

My brother Jeremy and his wife Kate said they would assist, so I would do the coursework, write out my essays longhand and they would type them up for me. They also read all the coursework themselves so that they understood the essays, but even with all that background knowledge they still sometimes had no idea what a word I had written was, between the handwriting and the spelling. I passed the course and Kate and Jeremy thought that they should have been given a DipEd as well after going through it all with me.

Diploma aside, we still don't take a prescriptive approach to pattern cutting and like to think of ourselves more as problem solvers than teachers. It's not just about laying down the rules of cutting and making the students adhere to them, it's about being responsive to how they learn and encouraging them to throw away the rulebook. Each student I work with comes to me with a different problem and part of my role is to react to this in a creative way. It's about thinking outside the box, being fearless with the conceptual pieces and leading the students to creative solutions. I don't appreciate laziness so heaven help a student who lacks application but I never give up on them and often find enthusiastic helpers from other years who are happy to be involved. Occasionally the reason a student is lagging could be due to personal tragedy, stress or a physical impairment and I always strive to find a way to surmount any obstacles.

The alchemy of teaching at Central Saint Martins is around the connection between the design concept and the final piece. It's important for the student to choose the right fabric for their designs but quite often they choose the wrong one and even though we tell them, they persist, so then we have to find a way to make it work. It could be material as diverse as an exquisite silk screen print on sheer georgette or an architectural structure in wood ply, which is then arranged around the human body. As a tutor of both design and pattern cutting, I have to think creatively about how individual students can achieve their best outcome. One of my strengths is to think on my feet, honed after years of working with the bizarre demands of advertising and film costume. I relish sitting down with a student to work out which material would be best for their project, whether it is a tent embellished with crystals to float over the model's head or choosing between a heavy grosgrain or corduroy for a mannish suit.

My school year begins with teaching the basic skills and is then defined by the different projects I teach across every year group. I work with the first years on the White Project, where they are given three themes – art, borderlines and lovers – from which they must pick one and they have three types of white fabric to use – stretch, cotton and fake suede. Through this process I teach them the relevant skills needed and unlock the doors to the pattern block cupboard. This is an archive of patterns amassed over many years so I'm strict about how they are borrowed and returned.

Under my guidance the students design their garment, make a toile, do a fitting, produce the final piece and then bring it to the crit, where they are marked. Not only will they learn a lot from the appraisal but so too will the rest of the class and I never fail to gain something either. That is one of the things I love about teaching. Everyone is learning, the students from the lecturers and from their fellow course mates and us, the lecturers, from our students. This project always ends with a catwalk show, which is designed and organised by the fashion journalism students. One year it was staged at the Royal Albert Hall but usually the students make use of the walkways around the college building – something Willie Walters sanctioned during her tenure. During the pandemic we taught online and the final year students graduating in 2020 made a film instead of a catwalk show. In 2021, the final year could only show one garment which they were advised to wear themselves as there was only one person allowed due to self-distancing. It was fantastic to see students, rather than models, in their pieces.

In the spring term I work with the first years on their pattern cutting project, the second years on their tailoring project and with the final years on their collections. At the end of the summer term, I also work with the second years on a special event, a favourite of mine. It's the annual collaboration with Grayson Perry, Chancellor of University of the Arts London (UAL – six colleges, of which CSM is one), on which I work alongside my colleague Natalie Gibson. Natalie is fabulously exotic and completely unique – she is great to work with and so supportive. The word 'iconic' is bandied around a lot these days but that is exactly what she is. She has been teaching print (and every other kind of embellishment on fabric) at CSM since 1965. In 1981 she became the Head of Fashion Print and she has taught many students who went on to have distinguished careers in fashion houses around the world. One of her most illustrious graduates is Sarah Burton, who took over as creative director at Alexander McQueen in 2010 following the tragic death of the house's creator.

Natalie's network of fashion and art contacts are unparalleled (as you may expect after a career longer than mine!), but she is just as energetic and focused on the new students. She is globally renowned for her expertise in the craft of fabric design and has even acted as a technical expert in court cases. Although beautifully flamboyant and colourful in appearance, she is very modest and doesn't talk about herself – she is just universally adored! Furthermore, she has the best desk of us all – a vintage wooden number which she brought over from the old building – piled high with fabrics, designs, accessories, old photographs and random objects so she can't sit at it or find her computer.

It was Natalie who got Grayson Perry interested in the work CSM were doing. They were old friends and she bumped into him on the bus on her way to work and he ended up coming into the school and having coffee. Natalie mentioned how brilliant her students would be at designing an outfit for him and suggested a project, which he thought was a marvellous idea. He called her a few months later and said, 'Are we going to do this or not?' and that was about 16 years ago – it's been running ever since.

I work with Natalie on the annual event which the second years take part in, designing an outfit for Grayson's female alter ego, Claire. Grayson starts the ball rolling by giving the students a vague brief; he's very open to whatever they design but there are a few stipulations – for example, he is not a big fan of leopard print or raw edges. That said, he is always happy to be persuaded if the piece works. He comes in every week throughout the process for fittings and pays for fabrics – it's such a wonderful experience for the students and we love having him around, he's fab to work with. The final event is like a crit, where Grayson models each outfit on the catwalk and he brings accessories – shoes and tights – with him to wear too. It's pure cabaret as he shimmies to the music each student has chosen for him! They also have their photo taken with Grayson in their outfit for inclusion in their portfolios and he always buys several of the dresses too, pinning gold envelopes to those he would like to purchase.

One year, our event fell the day after Brexit was voted in

and we were worried about the uncertainty of what might happen – he bought every dress! The three prizewinners get a ceramic 'Claire' statuette in gold, silver and bronze – a bit like the Oscars. Grayson regularly wears the student-designed clothes publicly and makes sure they have attached a label so he can credit them – he's a brilliant supporter of new talent. He is also appreciative of the staff on this project and one year, he gave us each a ceramic gold animal that he had made himself. I received a crow-like bird but he spotted it had a fault so he said he would make me another one. I offered to give the original back to him but he said, 'Oh no, keep it,' and then he made me a second, so I now have two original Grayson Perry pieces. Can you imagine? They are precious possessions, not just because they are stunning and made by him but because they represent the special relationship we all have through this project.

During their final year, the Print students stage a fashion show of their pre-collection – a practice run of their collection made in toile – for their tutors and peers just before Christmas. They are responsible for organising the models, hair, make-up, show space and music. For his final year on the BA in 2008/09, Craig Green (now one of the UK's highest-rated independent menswear designers) persuaded a group of Eastern European street musicians to provide the music. They played traditional instruments similar to small bagpipes, which were supposed to carry the sound effectively in the open air. In the Charing Cross tutorial room the noise was deafening but it created such an exciting show ambience! This alternative entertaining approach was typical of Craig. On the BA course, he started to develop his 3D-constructed shapes around the body using materials like lightweight wood. At first, he was unsure if this would be acceptable on a fashion course, however he was completely encouraged by me, Patrick and Natalie – we all loved this development.

Every so often we have a little celebration with champagne and snacks after a crit or event, like the White Project. One year, this got a little out of hand. It was incredibly hot and airless in the workspace and I made a comment about how uncomfortable it was. Patrick Lee Yow was with us and he had to pop out. When he returned, he was faced with the students marching around the room with marker pens scrawling 'we need air' on the walls and even the windows. He had left me alone for a moment and now look what had happened! The following morning, there was quite a rumpus and students were interviewed to find out if they had been involved and even had their pencil cases checked for the offending pens. Patrick and I thought we may be sacked. The complaints were taken to Willie Walters, who declared she was horrified. Except her disapproval was based on the graffiti being such poor quality, they really could have done better! She also said she would not pay for the walls to be cleaned when there were so many more important things to spend money on. What started in my print workspace has spread out across the fashion department and I love to see the students leave their mark – it's a lasting memory of them for me and adds to the vibrancy and energy of the place.

What's a design student without a little art anarchy?

Patrick says I'm a rebel. We will often disagree about a student or a situation but we engage in great discussions and one of us always compromises. He says that sometimes I'm like 'a dog with a bone' or I have 'a bee in my bonnet' but he is just as committed to getting to the crux of things, particularly if a student is suffering. The hardest moment is when we have to stand back and let them find their way rather than shoving them too hard in one direction. It's a little like not interfering with nature but being on hand to observe.

I'm lucky that I get to step into the student's journey at various points and it's a privilege to catch up with how much they have grown and be a small influence in the direction they take. I have been to Tokyo a couple of times, first with Natalie Gibson when we met up with past students and went to a restaurant where the chef gave me a top that the waiters wore – it was multi-coloured with fish, lobsters and Japanese writing on. More recently, Patrick and I were in Tokyo and we hooked up with old students and went to the same restaurant. This time the chef gave me the white top that the chefs wore! It was also wonderful to see them all again and although those students had left CSM, the experience had stayed with them – yet again proof that the network continues beyond the course. The college is a bit like taking out life membership and this is reassuring for students who navigate through a brutal industry. They keep in touch with us, the tutors, and their fellow graduates and we are there to advise, support and applaud.

Occasionally a student comes along and there is a special connection. Ashish Gupta is a great example of this. I mentioned him earlier in this book and am now returning to his story and our ongoing collaboration.

When Ashish graduated in 2000, he wanted to work in Paris but, just like a scene in a movie, he was on the phone at Gare du Nord railway station when his portfolio was stolen. It was a devastating moment. This was before the age of digital so all his work was lost and he had no choice but to return to London. He had nothing to show to designers and brands so instead he decided to set up his own thing. He started small and got in touch to ask if I would help him with pattern cutting and as a general sounding board to help navigate through the industry. I have been with him ever since and he now sells his designs all over the world and was honoured with a retrospective fashion show – Fashion In Motion – at the V&A Museum in 2015.

My relationship with Ashish is a true collaboration. We have worked together so well for so long that we understand what the other one means without needing to say too much. It reminds me of the shorthand I had with the Swanky Modes gang. There are always hurdles to overcome and we both revel in finding creative ways to deal with them. I work on every collection and make sure my diary is organised around his S/S and A/W timings – luckily, it fits with my teaching timetable. Ashish will get in touch with thoughts for the new season and then we will meet up to discuss his preliminary ideas, look at sketches and talk about fabrics. I developed a block (a basic shape to cut different patterns from) and we have created signature shapes which we refine every season as well as working on the new stuff too. I will take the designs away with me, cut the patterns which are made up in toile and then go along to the initial fittings – I often employ ex-students to come and help with the cutting and toiles.

After the show, we get together for a debrief and make any final changes before the collection is released into the wild. This has been our routine since 2001 and, although we may occasionally disagree on a sleeve length or a print, we have never argued. I know how much Ashish values me and the feeling is mutual – I have the utmost respect for him and his work. It is unusual for a pattern cutter to work exclusively with one designer so I know how lucky I am to be in this position still, after 20 years and many more ahead of us, I hope.

When I went back to Central Saint Martins I thought it would feed my desire to learn, satisfy my need to teach, keep me connected to beloved friends and colleagues and, crucially, be a lot of fun. It has been all those things and more, and although I never expected to still be there 20 years later, here I am and happily so. Willie's daughter Tamsin is here now too. We often meet up during the day and check in on each other, as we do with other colleagues. We really are one big fashion family and the lifeblood of the college operation. Age is just a number here; it means nothing whether you are in your twenties or seventies. I have heard people question the value of senior lecturers in an industry where youth, innovation and reinvention are prized above all else and it makes my blood boil! Being current and relevant has nothing to do with how old you are, it is an attitude to the job and world you operate in with a desire to keep learning. I hope I give my students the benefit of my knowledge and my enthusiasm but also instil in them a hunger to keep learning – what better example to set them?

The Art of Pattern Cutting

THE FIRST GARMENT I made, at the age of seven, was a gathered skirt although I didn't use a pattern. I was given measurements which I transferred directly onto the fabric before I cut the sections out and sewed them together. This is an ancient approach to making clothes, reflected in pieces like kimonos, sarongs and interesting trousers, and it's all about shapes – squares and rectangles – and size dictated by the width of the fabric. It is much less common nowadays but it absolutely fascinates me. I love to discover more about these types of garments, the cultures that use them so imaginatively and the way pieces of fabric are draped and folded. When I was in Indonesia, I bought several sarongs and I have picked up some in Brick Lane too. I love the variety of sari fabrics and make shirts and cardigans out of them.

I was a teenager when I used a pattern for the first time and made a waistcoat and skirt but, in all honesty, I didn't make a very good job of it. I was rushing because I wanted to wear the outfit to go out that night – which sounds a bit mad when I say it in these times. Back then, people would often make something or alter an outfit for a party. I didn't really care if it was still trailing threads or was ill-fitting so long as I had it for the event.

I learnt pattern cutting from one of my Swanky Modes partners, Judy Dewsbury, who had been taught by the legendary fashion designer Antony Price when she was at Royal College, and this ignited a lifelong obsession for me. When I joined CSM in 1999 and worked with Patrick Lee Yow, my fellow lecturer, I continued to learn from his traditional education in the art of pattern cutting. So, while I'm technically untrained, I learnt from the best and honed my craft over years of constant practice. I also chose to challenge the rules on cutting and the preconceptions of how something is done – asking *why* is important and trying alternatives means using intuition, which benefits the process. I have now been pattern cutting for 50 years and I'm *still* learning new things – from my own mistakes, from my peers and from working with the students I teach.

Pattern cutting is one of the most important elements in the design process. It's vital the cutter understands and interprets the designer's drawings and can translate them into garments. This is incredibly hard to do well and requires attention to detail, stamina and methodical spirit. It's the starting point for many garments in the fashion industry, whether they are mass produced or made-to-measure pieces, and for the home sewer they are a vital resource. In both cases, if you don't get the early stages right then you won't get the piece you were hoping for. That said, and I have said it before, once you know the techniques you can subvert them and have fun messing around.

A pattern is a two-dimensional template, designed to make something three-dimensional out of fabric. Cut for a specific size, it can be used repeatedly. It's a hugely important tool for us. I lock my pattern cupboard at Central Saint Martins and I'm strict about how the patterns are borrowed, where they are and that they are returned as soon as someone has stopped using them.

The most common pattern making is using an existing pattern but there are alternatives, like draping fabric on a stand, drafting freehand, digital techniques or using a garment that you can then copy from, called 'reverse engineering'. With a flat pattern you have a front and back, which can then be pinned onto the fabric you have chosen before carefully cutting it out. It is always advisable to make a mock-up first out of calico, which creates a toile. This can then be fitted to a person or a tailor's dummy before you tackle any alterations. Digital pattern design is mainly used for mass manufacturing. This isn't something I could ever consider. Apart from my disinterest in anything technological, I like to see and touch the patterns, I want to see the construction and create it, like a sculptor would with a block of stone. My favourite pattern cutting task is when I'm making something for the first time – it's as much about problem solving as it is about creating.

There has been a welcome resurgence in acknowledge-ment and respect for what we pattern cutters do. As CSM's Professor of Fashion History and Theory Alistair O'Neill says in his book, *Exploding Fashion: Making, Unmaking, and Remaking Twentieth Century Fashion*, 'The pattern cutter uses skills, knowledge, experience and judgment, often with untested and unfamiliar combinations of elements that require intellectual, practical and tacit knowledge and synthesis to interpret and resolve in a feasible manner.'

I couldn't have put it better myself!

The equipment needed includes a pencil (HB or H),

glue stick, magic tape, eraser, tracing wheel, set square or pattern master ruler, tape measure, colour crayons or felt tip pens, pins and weights. Whatever level you are, from the beginner to the professional, pattern cutting requires absolute attention. I would encourage you to give it a go if you haven't already and start with a simple bought pattern. If you are already well versed and itching to stretch your knowledge then try creating your own pattern. I have included a few of my golden rules below to bear in mind.

MY TOP TIPS FOR PATTERN CUTTING

1. Lay the pattern on the fabric and match the grain line on the pattern so it lines up parallel to the selvedge (edge of the fabric). Years ago, I was making a dressing gown in crepe de Chine for a commercial and I did it by eye in a rush, resulting in the front not hanging properly. I forget what the commercial was for but I will never forget the mistake I made and have not made it since.

2. Notches are marks that tell you how the pieces go together. It's important to mark notches on but I don't snip through the seam allowance because it's easy to cut it too long, meaning you end up with a hole – I always chalk my notches.

3. If you're using your own pattern, I would recommend giving it a name or a number and don't forget to

mark the grain and notches and write instructions directly onto the pattern for future reference. If you're using a readymade pattern, follow the instructions. This might sound obvious but it's amazing how many times we all think we know better, whether it is with sewing, a recipe or putting flat-pack furniture together!

4. Have patience and be methodical and meticulous. Even after 50 years, I'm still cautious and take a systematic approach – I'm never tempted to cut corners (literally!).

5. You can pin your pattern to the fabric if it is paper but if it is cardboard then I would use weights, particularly on fine fabric, to draw around. This also limits the risk of movement.

6. Draw around the pattern with chalk and then cut it out – you will get a more accurate result.

7. Always cut out on the wrong side of the fabric unless you are matching it. This avoids unwelcome marks on the right side.

8. Keep the fabric flat for as long as possible (the same applies when you are not using it) and stick to a certain order of construction, particularly for the

fiddly bits – ie. if you are fixing a pocket on, do so when the fabric is still flat, if possible.

9. If you are making a mock-up – toile – first, use a cheaper material that is close to the final fabric as the way it hangs can make a big difference.

10. Whether you have used a bought pattern or made your own, the toile should be fitted to you by someone else. It's hard to alter something when you're wearing it so ask a sewing friend to help.

11. As you gain more confidence, you can adapt a bought pattern or create your own. Alternatively, take a garment and unpick it to make a pattern that you can then replicate from. Sometimes it's easier to start with something in 3D, which is why I often use the draping technique, and it's how my students first learn. Again, it's important to mark the grain line before you start draping. You can get a cheap stand and pad it out into the right shape (if you need a female silhouette, add a bra and stuff it!).

12. Keep all the pattern pieces together and store carefully in the packet or a clearly marked envelope.

13. The more you do, the more confident and better you will get!

CHAPTER 9

The Great British Sewing Bee

J ust at the point some are thinking of retirement, I took on what has arguably been the biggest challenge of my career. It started with a party. A colleague and friend Sarah Gresty, BA Fashion Course Leader, from Central Saint Martins (who took over from Willie Walters), was celebrating her 50th birthday and I got chatting to a lovely guest. We had the standard 'So what do you do?' conversation and she said she was a TV producer and was working on a new sewing programme. I told her what I did and she asked if I would have been interested in being part of it, to which I said absolutely, but she said they thought they had found someone. I thought no more of it.

When the first series of the BBC's *The Great British Sewing Bee* aired in 2013 I was thrilled that the craft and sewing industries were so well represented by the production, the judges Patrick Grant and May Martin, the presenter Claudia Winkleman and the contestants. At last there was a mainstream programme focused on designing, pattern cutting, altering and sewing clothes.

After three series of the show, the producers wanted to make it more fashion focused and began a search for a new judge with a design background. They cast their net wide, including many designers, but the producer I had met at the party remembered our conversation and asked the team to get in touch with CSM and enquire after me. Willie Walters spoke to them and put us in touch. She told them I was teaching the pattern cutting course and I think she may have described me as the ultimate expert but whatever it was she said, it worked because they asked me to come and meet them.

I met the executive producer, Susanne Rock, and her team at the production company, Love Productions, for an informal interview in 2015. I was rather nervous, which is an unusual feeling for me – I was out of my comfort zone and transported into a world I had only ever seen from one angle, as that of the costume maker the other side of the camera. But they soon put me at my ease and we talked about my career, knowledge and passion for design so by the time I left, I knew I couldn't have done any more and whatever happened next was meant to be. I had nothing to lose. When they called me back for the next stage of the interview process my nerves returned and I realised how much I wanted it.

In advance of the interview, they wanted me to send them my Curriculum Vitae. Well, I knew what a CV was, but I had never needed one before in my life. I had always found work through colleagues and collaborators, many of whom who had worked with us at Swanky Modes, who then called me when their careers had developed. I called my brother Jeremy. He had needed to write his own CV reasonably often when going for a new job, but he thought that the style of CV he was used to writing might not really hit the spot for me: 'What you need is lots of pictures,' he said. So, my CV was half text covering Swanky Modes, adverts and films, and teaching, and half pictures of the outfits – it looked rather good!

In the second interview I was asked to critique two sewers who were working on pieces in the studio. My confidence flooded back. I was being asked to do something I did every day as a lecturer at Central Saint Martins and I was completely at home in this environment – giving honest feedback, sharing useful tips and activating my laser stare! Again, I left feeling that I had given it my all but this time around the stakes were higher because now I really wanted the job.

I was through to the final stage of the process, which meant an audition with Patrick Grant, the existing judge, to find out if we had any chemistry. I knew Patrick by his fantastic reputation only so I reasoned, if all else failed, at least I got to meet him and show him around Central Saint Martins. We were filmed together and got on immediately. Patrick and I have had very different journeys through the industry but there are many similarities to the way we work and I know he appreciates the history and knowledge I share. The producers cut together some footage of us, showed it to the BBC and the rest is history.

Susanne has since told me they knew, the instant they

met me, that I was the one they wanted, which is very kind of them. Apparently my 'mischievous honesty' convinced them that I was right for the show as well as my 'humour, eagle eye for mistakes, exacting standards, excellence at detail and great taste'. I know this sounds like I'm blowing my own trumpet but after a childhood of wishy-washy school reports, it's a lovely validation from a team I hugely respect. I might even print the words on a T-shirt! Okay, I'm joking … or am I …?

Accepting the position of judge on the programme was a big adventure at this point in my career. I could have taken it easy and continued to teach at college part-time and make costume for rest of the time but where would be the jeopardy in that? I like to try new and different things and I think it's wonderful that I had the opportunity to start a new career when I was nearly 70!

⊗ ⊗ ⊗

On my first filming day I was a heady mix of nerves and excitement as I walked onto the set. Not that anyone guessed – they thought I was very calm and collected, I was later told. The production crew, Patrick Grant and Claudia Winkleman could not have been more welcoming and immediately put me at ease. Claudia was so down to earth – open and helpful – and was like that with everyone on set. In fact, Claudia's mum, the newspaper editor Eve Pollard, had written about Swanky Modes back in the day so she knew a little of my history too.

I don't mean this how it sounds, but I have no problem being in front of the camera – it really doesn't bother me. As long as I'm doing something I'm confident in – like design and sewing – then I'm not frightened of being filmed; if anything, I enjoy it. On the very first show, I commented on a garment one of the contestants had made, asking the model to turn around before saying, 'It fits really well under her arse. It's sexy.' I thought no more of it but the producers called it a 'spitting out your tea moment' because they didn't expect me to say that and they kept it in the show. They thought it was an unexpected and brilliant way to set the tone of the new judge – I do say what I think!

The first series aired in 2016 and as I don't have a TV, I went around to Anne Martin and Suggs' house in Camden to watch it, along with a big gang of my old mates. I invited Susanne Rock, the producer, to join us too and she did, although I think she was initially surprised to be asked. I was embracing my second life – it's a surprising and thrilling new chapter.

The format of each show includes three challenges – the pattern task, the transformation and the made-to-measure. These are all areas I have been immersed in for over 50 years so I'm pretty well qualified to comment. I think being on the show has reminded me exactly how much I do know and there's the odd moment where I share a story with the team, like pulling out a roll of Lycra fabric and mentioning Swanky Modes were one of the first to make dresses out of it. The reaction to this threw me because the team thought this was groundbreaking and it made me realise that yes, it was! Sometimes it's easier to see what you have achieved when it's reflected in the faces of those you tell.

Every year the contestants are a fabulous bunch. They are full of focus, energy and excitement tinged with utter fear. Just stepping into the *Sewing Bee* workshop can be enough to make your knees weak and that's before the cameras, the timed challenges, the competitive nature of the show and us, the scary judges! I'm told that I'm the most feared but I can't quite see it myself. Like Patrick, I'm honest and I don't sugar-coat criticism or waste words. I don't dish out praise when I don't mean it because that's not going to help anyone. I'm also rather good at spotting the tiniest mistakes. It's one of my superpowers – I can detect issues from the other side of the room. And this leads me on to one of my pet hates: the cover-up. I don't mind a cover-up as long as they're so good they look meant, but I can tell when someone has made a mistake and attempts to disguise it with a pointless trim or a bow that's too big – it drives me mad. That's not to say that Patrick and I are strict, we spend time walking around the studio floor giving quiet words of encouragement and the occasional snippet of advice. The contestants are just as supportive of each other too, give practical help and often discuss the challenges, which is even more heartwarming considering they are in direct competition. It's a bonding experience – I think this is something sewing together encourages. Once the series is finished, they have a WhatsApp group to keep in touch and they also cross over with past contestants too so it's one big happy family across the years.

Working with Patrick is one of the joys of being part of the show. We entertain and amuse each other every day and have a mutual respect for our industry achievements and knowledge. We share a green room on set, where we can hang out and I play a lot of music – eighties, soul and reggae – things I can dance to. As you will know by now, I love to dance! Patrick says I play the music at 'ear-splitting volume' and he will turn it down while I am not looking but I think he rather likes my taste because he now has a playlist of my tunes. The production team asked if I had any requirements and I couldn't think of a single thing so they put a basket of sweets in the room and I'm now addicted to them. They take out the strawberry flavour and give them to someone else because they know they're not my favourite! That's my idea of spoilt. Plus, they include packets of Mini Cheddars. I don't eat snacks when I'm at home but in the middle of a long filming day, it's such a treat.

Patrick continues to oversee the running of his bespoke tailoring business when we are filming. We spend a lot of companionable time together, whether he is reading and I'm sewing, or he will do the crossword and I will tackle the sudoku – Patrick says we are like Jack Spratt and his wife! We also go for walks, lunch or a drink in the evening. We don't see each other much between series so when we're together, we enjoy the time we have. I think we make a rather good double act and our height difference amuses me – he's so tall and I'm so short – and I'm told it translates really well on screen.

I must confess that I don't watch myself, other than to check what I'm wearing, so I don't repeat outfits too close together because I like to reuse clothes. I don't need to see myself in action but I want to make sure I'm not wearing the same outfits from the previous series. It's the fashion designer in me. I will often alter or make a garment ready for the next episode, beavering away behind a sewing machine, and always like to have a project on the go. My long-term collaborator, Ashish Gupta, will often create something special for me – I have had the most amazing jumpers from him too. Big necklaces are a signature style for me and I enjoy making my own, like the statement piece I made out of mini hand sanitiser bottles, which I emptied and filled with different coloured dyes. I linked them together using carabiners from the set and turned them into a necklace. That was a nod towards lockdown and caused a bit of a stir on Twitter!

Amazingly, we were able to keep filming through the pandemic, which shows just how fantastic the production crew and the contestants are. Everyone was very patient and abided by the rules – it was particularly frightening before the vaccine but none of us wanted to put the show on hold. I don't think it's an exaggeration to say it was one of the programmes that the public needed and proved to be a popular distraction from real life. The *Sewing Bee* team tell me sales of sewing machines have gone up by 70 per cent and many more men are taking up sewing as a hobby – so brilliant! I know crafting and making has been a huge sanity saver during the lockdowns, underlined by the success of my pal Grayson Perry's *Grayson's Art Club* on Channel 4. I hope people continue to create – it's so good for our mental health, it promotes wellbeing, teaches us to problem solve and gives us a break from our screens.

After my first series, Claudia Winkleman left – I don't think that was my fault, just a coincidence! – and the comedian Joe Lycett took over. Patrick and I met Joe for the first time at the Hammersmith Apollo in 2018, after we had seen him perform. We loved it and I know Joe was buoyed by the exchange and hopeful that filming together would work out well. He now says the three years we worked together were 'a total delight in that happy little trio of mischief'. He and I connected immediately. In filming breaks I would entertain him with the occasional story from my life and make him laugh almost as much as he did me. I think he appreciates my attitude of approaching life with the intention of living it, saying yes to as many experiences as possible and rarely giving too much thought to what people might think or say.

I know Joe was unsure how Patrick and I would feel about some of the sillier sketches so imagine his surprise when we threw ourselves into it all – we have no problem looking a little daft. One of his favourites involved a sketch where it appeared he was being snowed on, before the camera panned out to reveal me grating Parmesan on his head from a short height! He has since said that I deliver the comedy lines from the sketches impeccably and have 'an invaluable instinct for dryness and not overselling a joke' – high praise indeed from my comedy icon.

We are great drinking partners too. I have perfected the delivery of, 'Oh gosh, not another one!' while simultaneously cracking open a bottle. Joe and I have had many happy nights wandering around London restaurants and bars. We had a brilliant *Sewing Bee* team lunch at an Italian restaurant to celebrate the end of Joe's first series. As Patrick and the producers gradually peeled away, we kept going, through the afternoon and into the evening. Joe was due to appear on Richard Herring's Leicester Square Theatre podcast that evening and he invited me along. I ended up in the front row next to Joe's friend, who very naughtily sent Joe a picture of me nodding off as he was being interviewed. I was just resting my eyes! It didn't last for long because I remember standing up and heckling them at one point in the recording and, luckily, both were highly entertained by the interruption. We then went on to the now-closed Café Monico on Shaftesbury Avenue to celebrate our joint performance with one more bottle.

I do have a bit of previous on the heckling front. My

niece Caroline does stand-up and when she's getting a show ready to go to the Edinburgh Festival Fringe I often go along to see how it's developing, and to give her some feedback. That's meant to be after the show, of course, but I sometimes get a bit carried away with it all and give her my feedback during the show – or as it is better known, I heckle her. Like a good comedian though, she sees it as an opportunity rather than a problem – in one show after I had offered a few comments from the audience she paused and turned to everyone and said, 'You probably won't believe this, but that's my auntie!'

One of the biggest laughs I gave Joe was a small remark I made, to myself, at the end of a long filming day. The days on set can be mercilessly long and we were just coming to the close of two days of intense filming. We were all struggling to stifle yawns and as soon as one yawned, it set the others off. We were standing in a line, waiting for the cameras to focus and the director to give the go-ahead when I let out an almighty yawn. Exhausted but still standing, I could feel the delirium beginning to set in. I thought I had told myself off in my head but instead, out loud, to the group I said, 'Stop yawning, you bitch!' You should have seen the soundman, he roared with laughter!

When Joe left the show we had a farewell meal after he had done his final voiceover session. It was a warm summer's evening and London was typically busy so after our dinner we were struggling to find a suitable watering hole. We happened to wander past The French House, which was heaving and everyone I was with despaired that we would ever find a place to sit. 'Don't worry,' I said, 'I know the proprietor, Lesley.' So, I popped in and gave her a wave. She came bustling out from behind the bar and forced an outdoor group of disparate ageing men nursing warm ales to concertina themselves down the table to make space for us.

My old Soho network coming up trumps again.

I loved working with Joe and miss him from the show but we are now friends for life, sharing a love of nights out, funny stories and art – he and his mum are wonderful artists and she drew my portrait, which I use as my Instagram picture! The comedienne Sara Pascoe has now stepped into his trainers and is proving to be just as fantastic a presenter and great company too.

I can't tell you how much I enjoy being part of *The Great British Sewing Bee* and they say they love me too which is nice to hear. The crew are wonderful and just as important as those of us in front of the camera. We have the same team each series, which has made us feel like a family. I treat everyone equally, from the runner to the executives and I think, of course, we all deserve the same respect. I have never bowed down to anyone or expected people to behave that way to me. I'm interested in others, in what they think, who they are and in finding connections between us when we talk. When I first became a judge on the show, a friend of mine, film producer and husband of my friend Rachael Fleming, Andrew Macdonald, said

I was 'going over to the other side now' after a lifetime of beavering away behind the camera.

⊗ ⊗ ⊗

The Sewing Bee was a new career in itself but has also opened up fresh avenues to me in television and radio as well as bringing in invitations to do talks and to support charity fundraising. The TV invitations have mainly been to appear on 'celebrity' quiz and panel shows. In my younger days I found that when I got home from a hard day at Swanky Modes I would just slump down in front of the TV and find myself completely mesmerised, no matter what was on, until broadcasting stopped for the evening. After a while I decided that since I didn't seem to have the willpower to stop watching once I'd started, I'd better get rid of the TV altogether and so I haven't had one now for over 45 years. As a result, I had no idea what these shows were all about that I was now being invited to appear on.

But what the hell? When a door swings open I'm always intrigued to know what's on the other side, so through this open door I stepped. While I take my work very seriously, I try not to take myself too seriously at all. Which is just as well when I'm appearing on shows that take me out of my comfort zone and sometimes a little out of my depth.

On the *Sewing Bee*, of course, I'm in my element, talking about something that I know a lot about and love, but on these quiz shows you just never know what might come up and my memory is not the best when it comes to answering general knowledge questions and of course it's definitely much harder when you're in front of an audience.

My high point so far – at least in terms of not making a complete arse of myself – was probably my appearance on Michael McIntyre's *The Wheel* on BBC1 in 2020. I somehow emerged as having answered more questions correctly than anybody else. How on earth did that happen? If I began to believe that I was a bit of a whiz on these shows because of that (actually, I didn't), I would have soon been brought down to earth by my appearance on BBC's *The Weakest Link* in 2021. It turned out that I was the very weakest of the weakest links, being the first contestant to be booted off. What humiliation! At least Patrick Grant went on to be the overall winner, thus saving the honour of the *Sewing Bee*. Amongst other things I also appeared on another BBC show, *Would I Lie to You?*, and I'm not sure that I was very good on that one either, as I'm not much of a liar. Maybe I didn't practise enough when I was younger. Mind you, I did tell the quite amusing (true) story about riding topless on the back of a motorbike (Chapter 4).

Generally speaking, I'm up for 'having a go' at most things on the basis that life is short and you may as well have a crack, but even so I don't accept absolutely everything that I'm offered. I was asked to appear on BBC's *Mastermind*, but no thank you, I'd have been like a rabbit in the headlights. And thank goodness I'll never be asked to appear on *University Challenge* – I don't want to come across as a complete nincompoop! However, when asked if I'd like to compete in *Celebrity Master Chef* in 2017, I was very, very tempted because I love cooking and I'm not at all bad at it, if I say so myself. I also thought that it would teach me a thing or two about the stresses and strains of being a contestant on such programmes and so give me an insight into the experience of the contestants on the *Sewing Bee*. After that, perhaps I would be a better judge – maybe not quite so pernickety!

But when I thought about it, it would have meant taking time out from my teaching at Central Saint Martins – perhaps quite a lot of time if I'd done well enough to make it through to the later rounds. When it came down to it, that was something that I was not prepared to do. I regard teaching as my 'real job' and it's not something that I want to jeopardise for the sake of a passing bit of entertainment. Apart from CSM being my 'core' employment, I also rely on it for a steady income to provide my bread and butter – to say nothing of the occasional glass of wine! I'm over 70 already, but I'll probably have to keep working until I drop because I don't have any pension that would allow me to sail off into the sunset. Not that I'm complaining about that. It's a bit of a cliché, but working with generation after generation of fresh-faced students has kept me young at heart. Some of their vitality, creativity and enthusiasm rubs off on me and that's what keeps me motivated.

So now I've found myself on the merry-go-round of 'celebrity' shows and this is a whole new world for me and it's quite fun. I'm going to enjoy the ride while it lasts because it probably won't be all that long before everyone has got a bit bored with me and I'll be cast aside like the proverbial old chip wrapper, so I take it all with a pinch of salt (and maybe a splash of vinegar!). But for now I'm spinning around and not getting too dizzy as the scenery whizzes past. And who knows, maybe before the spinning stops there's still a chance that I'll be invited on to a different sort of reality show – for example, *Who Do You Think You Are?* or one of those fly-on-the-wall jaunts for wrinkly 'celebs' to explore what life would be like in some far-flung place, *Best Exotic Marigold Hotel* style. I don't think that I would turn down stuff like that.

Now that I've carved out a niche for myself on the *Sewing Bee*, people seem much more interested in what I have to say than they ever were before, but of course I'm still just the same as I always was, for better or for worse. So, as well as the light-hearted 'celeb' shows, I now also get invited to do somewhat more serious-minded stuff, such as talks and radio. One of the first talks I was asked to do was in Norfolk, where I was invited by the organiser, who happened to be a fan of Swanky Modes. I also talked about my life at The Stitch Festival in London, which featured a selection of my work in a mini-exhibition. Due to the pandemic such events have been put on hold, but I look forward to doing more – as soon as Covid allows.

My first radio appearance was on BBC Radio 4's *Woman's Hour* in April 2020 to discuss sewing, fashion and sustainability, the latter issue coming more and more to the fore in recent years. And I appeared on Radio 4's *Saturday Live* in June 2021 with other panellists from very diverse backgrounds, which made for a fascinating conversation. Mind you, the fact that *Saturday Live* really does go out live unnerved me slightly, in case I made a complete pig's ear of things!

Amongst my efforts for charity, I knitted a scarf that was auctioned in 2020 to raise funds for Crisis, the homeless charity, and I was very pleased to be asked to contribute a couple of small paintings to an auction to raise money for the charity Combat Stress, the following year. Because of my own dad's experience of getting shot down and being very badly injured as a pilot in the Second World War, I feel that I have a personal connection to the issue and was honoured to be asked and to be able to do my small bit to help others who have had similar experiences in more recent times. Many better-known people than myself also contributed paintings, including sculptor Anish Kapoor and actress Joanna Lumley who is well known for her campaigning in support of the Gurkhas and whose own father served in the Gurkha regiment.

And talking of my dad, all of this reminds me of what he said when I was young – 'You can be whatever you want to be'. And who would have thought that the dreamy little girl who struggled to read due to her deafness would one day write a book? I think that he would be very proud of me and delighted with whatever successes I have had.

CHAPTER 10

Seams Like A Dream

How strange it is to reach the final chapter in the story of my life when I feel like I have so much of it still left to live! I have found this process of looking back over the years – from my childhood to very recent events – much harder, but also more rewarding, than I expected. There is so much I had forgotten and needed prompting on from my lovely family and fabulous friends, as well as reminders of a few moments I didn't want to linger on. It has highlighted the importance of Swanky Modes in the history of the British fashion industry and shown me how much I have achieved in the 50 years and counting that I have been in the business. I wanted this to be a cracking yarn for you, the reader, but also for me, as a full and accurate record of my life. As the director Steve McQueen said, 'The best thing about life is that we get to have memories.' Thank you for joining me here to share mine.

One of the things I am most proud of is being a pattern cutter. Ever since the early Swanky Modes days, shadowing Judy Dewsbury and learning the hard way by making mistakes, I have been a committed cutter. I remember Judy would tell me something had to be done in a certain way and I would ask why. And she would say, 'That's a very good point.' While the art of cutting is respected within the fashion industry it does not always have the kudos it should have in the wider world so when my colleague, the fashion historian and curator Alistair O'Neill, who teaches Fashion History and Theory at Central Saint Martins, asked me in 2018 to take part in a project he was working on, I jumped at the chance. He wanted to investigate the role of the pattern cutter through the eyes of curators, fashion historians and photographers and bring the worlds closer together. Part of the plan was for his research to be transformed into a beautiful coffee table book.

He chose five iconic dresses from the 20th century – Charles James and Halston located in New York, Vionnet and Balenciaga in Paris and Comme des Garçons in Kyoto – to use as examples for the project and invited Patrick Lee Yow and me to join him on his pilgrimage. This was a dream come true for a pattern cutter – to be allowed into the most hallowed museum archives housing incredible garments that are not on show to the public and pieces that I have only ever heard hushed talk of.

The collections assistants were excellent at their job of protecting and handling these items, due to their fragility and susceptibility to air temperature and skin contact. I completely respected their professionalism and the garments themselves but it was so frustrating not to be able to pick something up and move it around, turn it inside out and understand how it has been constructed. We certainly couldn't put the dresses on a human model or mannequin, we had to pick up on every little detail like a detective looking for clues and consider aspects such as the way the yarn might be running or an element of the fabric. Looking without touching is a difficult task and Patrick and I had to ask the assistants to move pieces in a certain way. They were very helpful and we bonded over our mutual obsession with dressmaking, which meant they trusted us enough to allow us to delve a little deeper. I think this came from their respect for us as pattern cutters: they recognised kindred spirits.

We were asked to make patterns of each and recreate them and so we reverse engineered the dresses by starting with the finished piece before taking measurements, creating patterns from them, making a toile and then constructing the piece in the final fabric. The data from this process was then given to a digital animation company who set up a motion session at Pinewood Studios. The fashion model was captured walking and then the dresses were digitally 'worn', creating film of the final pieces to see them come to life in a triumph of cutting-edge technology.

There were surprises along the way, like the designer Charles James' dress that we felt was at first glance badly finished. It appeared to be roughly executed and the industry had in the past accused him of disrespecting the cloth he was working with. He was best known for his ballgowns and was more of a sculptor, with a reputation for roughly treating the fabric to make it do what he wanted. It was only when we looked more closely at the garment and began to make our own version that we realised it wasn't a bodge job at all and the techniques he had used were what had enabled him to create the finished piece. We all had so much more respect for him as a designer after that.

As well as seeing the Charles James' dress when we were in New York, we looked at the Halston too. Being there reminded me of a time I had visited the city in the early seventies with a friend and we met up with an artist friend of his in Long Island. The artist lived in a stunning modern house in the middle of the field which was pretty special but then he invited us for a swim at his neighbour's. By the swimming pool and littered around the garden were incredible sculptures by Henry Moore and Alberto Giacometti – my eyes were out on stalks!

There were several standout moments from our museum trips. One of them was meeting the curator, fashion historian and author Pamela Golbin at the Musée des Arts Décoratifs in Paris and seeing pieces from the collection of the French designer Madeleine Vionnet. Arguably one of Europe's leading couturiers, Madeleine Vionnet is considered the creator of the bias-cut style, where the fabric is cut at an angle of 45 degrees to the selvedge to give it stretch – the finer the fabric, the more it stretches. Being so close to her work was a dream come true and I was in awe of her design and the quality of the sewing. Pamela Golbin was charming and very interested in Patrick's and my views. It was unsurprising to hear that Vionnet relied on an army of dressmakers – behind every great designer is a great pattern cutter (or between 40 and 50 in Madeleine's case!). There is no collection without an army of technicians and their part of the process should be celebrated. Alistair felt that Patrick and I personified that and he included our conversations in the final chapter of his book for posterity, which was a lovely thing to do.

When we were in the middle of research at the V&A Museum in London I asked if I could take a look at the Swanky Modes 'Amorphous' dress they have there in the archives – it was wonderful to see it and know that it is safely preserved there.

We are a part of fashion history too.

It was absolutely brilliant to go behind the scenes and also to recreate the iconic pieces, using fabrics as close to the originals as possible. We had donations from cloth manufacturers too. The most difficult to match was the wool jersey because modern wool jersey is much more stretchy than its historical relation.

Each of the outfits posed their own challenges. The Halston was difficult because it was chiffon, so it had to be beautifully sewn as the material is unforgiving to any tiny mistakes. The fabric wasn't wide enough so we had to decide where to place the seam to make sure it wouldn't be spotted and we tucked it in the tie at the front of the dress. The Vionnet, made of georgette, required a serious systematic approach because it was made up of two rectangles with a series of folds in different directions. Plus, one sleeve had to be sewn on and one wasn't. The Balenciaga was the most complicated pattern, while the Comme des Garçons, even though at first the pattern seemed fairly simple, made up of two rectangles, was really hard to put together. The Charles James' pattern was complex to cut as all the pieces had to have the grain of the material in the same direction otherwise as the light fell on the dress, the various sections would look as if they were different colours. It took three of us four hours to cut! I loved each garment we worked on. It was impossible to choose a favourite and it was fascinating to hear the stories behind them and about their creators too.

The finished book – *Exploding Fashion: Making, Unmaking and Remaking Twentieth Century Fashion* by Alistair O'Neill – was published in November 2021 and it's an exquisite, informative and unique insight into the world of pattern cutting, full of incredible photographs. Alistair has done the most amazing job and it's a triumph of a book. It's been an immense privilege to have been involved, taken those trips and investigated such iconic pieces with Patrick. There's a photo in the book which sums me up as a pattern cutter, I think: I'm on the pattern cutting table, actually on it on my knees, with a pair of scissors and a rotary cutter. I wouldn't usually use a rotary cutter but because the fabric was so fine, I used it on the straight lines and then switched to the scissors on the corners. I had to put four tables together to create a big enough space that avoided the fabric hanging over the edges as it needed to be flat, but then of course I couldn't reach because I'm quite small. I could only get the right angle by climbing on the table. And that, my friends, is the attitude one must have to cut a pattern correctly – whatever it takes!

Unlike my 60th, I didn't have a party for my 70th birthday, although I did have a series of celebrations with friends and family. In my family we don't really do birthday presents, except on the decades, although we're a bit haphazard at that too, so I wasn't necessarily expecting anything. A dinner with my family was arranged at Pique Nique, which was the restaurant where the *Sewing Bee* contestants were filmed having their coffee or tea between challenges in one series. My brother Jeremy suggested that we should meet for a glass of fizz beforehand at Eames Fine Art, a nearby gallery he knew. It was just us and Christy from their staff, who I had met when I went to see the band she sings with at a gig with Jeremy.

Jeremy suggested that as we were in the Eames Fine Art Gallery it might be nice to look at their exhibition and so we moved round the gallery, discussing them in turn. 'What do you think of the next one?' asked Jeremy. 'What! That's my beach hut!' I exclaimed and everyone burst into fits of laughter. Natalie Gibson, who I work with at CSM, is married to Jon Wealleans, the artist and architect, and my siblings had asked him to paint a picture of my hut for my birthday. Then they had hung it in amongst an exhibition and the gallery were all in on the surprise. Such a nice present, and done so well. It's now hanging in pride of place in my flat.

After the wonderful success of my 60th birthday trip to Iran, my brother Chris has proposed that we drive to Ulan Bator in Mongolia in his 30-year-old clapped-out banger of a Rover Metro, which seems to be held together by sticky tape and moss.

I have yet to be persuaded.

My work life changed, like many others, in the pandemic. Lockdown meant teaching online, which was incredibly hard for everyone because of the nature of such a physical, tactile subject. I was quite impressed with myself, considering I'm not very good at technology! Louis Loizou suggested I buy a small tripod for my phone. I had half scale blocks so I could then demonstrate, step by step, to the students on Teams. In between lockdowns, we managed to return to the college so I could touch base with students and then when we were allowed back properly, the attendance was restricted to three days a week. We have all found a way to make it work and continue at the same high standard as before. Some of the catwalk shows and events have suffered but the excellent attitudes of the tutors and students remain.

One side effect of the pandemic was that I took a

walk every day in the largely deserted city. I discovered interesting parts of London, aged alleyways, fascinating monuments and pieces of architecture. I particularly liked the contrast between the old and the new, sitting side by side. I also rediscovered my love of photography, which I had enjoyed so much at art school, and got great pleasure from thinking about the composition of my photos, rather than just taking snaps. Instagram gave me a platform to share them, and some positive feedback, but mostly, I just enjoyed the process of composing the image.

I juggle all three elements of my career on a weekly and sometimes daily basis. I'm a lecturer, a designer and now also a TV judge (or personality if you like) so each day can take a different tone and direction. It keeps me fulfilled, focused and full of life! Recently I was asked to audition for the role of a seamstress in a big TV period drama. I know that sounds mad as I'm not an actress, or would have wished to be one, but when the opportunity arose I thought, well, why the hell not? So I did. It was a Zoom audition and I gave it a go but I didn't get it. I should have asked my actor friend and Natalie Ward's partner, Sam Spruell, to rehearse it with me and give me some tips but I didn't think too hard about it at the time. If there was another chance at some point I might go for it because I can't resist being thrown a new challenge.

I still share a workshop with Natalie Ward and Liza Bracey, both hugely successful costume designers and fabulous studio colleagues. I have about a quarter of it and they have the rest for their studio space and housing their extensive costume wardrobe. I keep a lot of my collections there too, including some of Swanky Modes and my vast vintage lingerie haul. Renting costumes out has paid for the space, which is a lovely, serendipitous thing. I will always need a studio, it's the foundation of what I do and a chance to reconnect if I've been away teaching or filming. The buzz of actors coming in for fittings, catching up with Natalie and Liza or sitting quietly behind my machine, working away on something, is as important to me as any of the other work I do.

Swanky Modes feels like 20 years ago, not 50, when we first started. It appears all the time in one way or another, whether an interview, a conversation or a garment resurfacing – like Rachael Fleming sending me a photo of her university student daughter Sylvie wearing an old Swanky Modes skirt that Rachael used to wear when she worked for us. It's a very short denim number with double zips at the front and a woven badge on the back pocket depicting two people walking around the planet Earth. My sister-in-law Kate also still wears a Swanky Modes outfit – a long sleeved polo neck dress made of stretched crushed grey velvet – and tells me she often gets compliments on it. I love to see these pieces being worn and the passing on of them from generation to generation – I know Mel Langer's daughter Isla Wickham and Willie Walters' daughter Tamsin Walters delve in to the archives too.

Fashion has changed so much over the years I have been in the industry and yet it has that cyclical quality, with younger generations plundering the archives and using old designs to inform new details. I do think that it's so much harder for kids coming into this business now. When I started, it was more about the independents than the chain stores and we didn't need huge investment to get started. London shop rents were relatively affordable and we could take risks because the mistakes weren't prohibitively expensive. Also, mass production has really changed how things are made. Now there are bigger questions too around the environmental issues we face and the future of fashion. I have read in various articles that the clothing industry is the second-biggest polluter after oil. That's gobsmacking. We need to turn the tide on our throwaway culture, buy less, wear what we have, look after our clothes and mend them. A good option is to think of different combinations so that each time you wear a piece you give it a new twist because of what you have paired it with. If you want to be sustainable, start with the clothes that you have already got. It's an incredibly complicated issue and as possible solutions arise, they bring their own pitfalls – like hiring outfits and accessories, which seems a sensible option until you think about the dry cleaning needed each time they are returned. There are no easy answers but the fashion industry must engage with it – and fast.

I am fascinated by how things are made in different eras and across the centuries. My research always informs my design. It's what we did at Swanky Modes, like when we looked at the 1930s bias-cut revolution and reimagined it as a bodycon design in Lycra. Both styles give the same end result, to accentuate the shape. I don't tend to go to charity shops for clothes now as they generally come from eras I have lived through. I still have a fabulous collection of my mum's 1960s wardrobe and I've given pieces to Isla, which she wears. While I would still buy vintage up to the 1950s, I don't look later than that. I think this is to do with wearing things first time around: they lose their appeal on the second time and I certainly wouldn't wear eighties fashion now – I never really liked the *Dynasty* look. That said, if I found something special – like the Valentino knitted lurex jumper with giant shoulders I unearthed a few years ago – I would grab it! I'm eternally on the lookout for sewing books as I have a library of vintage sewing books that I rarely have time to look at but love having, so I do pop into charity shops. I have a keen eye for jewellery and underwear for my collection too.

You will be pleased to hear that I'm just as close to all my siblings as I was when we were growing up. My sister Fiona was taught sewing by Sister Helen at school, the same nun who taught me, but it's only after she married that she has become more interested in textiles and machine knitting. She once made a jumper with a Christmas tree on the front for her daughter, Caroline, who flatly refused to wear it! Fiona started experimenting with plastic and wire and took a textile course at Morley College in London, where she made a dress out of steel and knitted wire. She also took part in an amateur knitting competition organised by the V&A, where the entrants chose a museum object to inspire a piece of work – she made a ballet dress based on a Swedish glass bowl and won a prize! Fiona is part of the Carousel textile artists group and they regularly hold exhibitions, one of which was in the library at the Barbican. She makes fabulous jewellery too from wire, plaster of paris and fabrics and I keep nagging her to make me a necklace to wear on *The Great British Sewing Bee*.

As well as my fantastic brothers and sister, I now have four adult nieces. Fiona has two daughters – Caroline, who went to art school and then studied animation at Royal College before becoming a stand-up comedian and broadcaster, and Sarah, who went to Cambridge, then to Imperial College, before going out to Africa and India to help set up solar energy. After she had children, she took up teaching at the NCT. Angus also has two daughters – Alice, who loved ballet as a child (I made her a Minnie Mouse outfit which her little daughter now wears) and who dabbled in pattern cutting before becoming a successful jewellery maker, and Olivia, who studied psychology at Kent University before becoming a jewellery maker and working for Anya Hindmarch, where she is also a brilliant embosser. I would often make them fancy-dress clothes when they were little and then several outfits as they grew up, like the dress I made for Sarah's May Ball at university and Alice's wedding dress. I'm very proud of my nieces –

Charlotte, Rebecca, Maddie, Lois and Cecelia – and one great nephew – Owen.

As well as my own family, I have the Swanky Modes gang and their children. Isla, Mel's daughter, has always been a particularly important part of my life and the closest thing I have to a daughter of my own. Now she has a daughter, Jess, and I adore her too. On the wall in my sitting room I used to measure Isla and draw a line of how tall she was and marked me on there too. When I painted the room, I left a square so the heights are still there, including mine, which Isla has long grown past!

I would take Isla away on camping holidays, taking our bikes on the train, heading for adventure and we would make a diary and both draw things we saw, like animals, insects and plants – a holiday journal. We did the same when we went to Mexico together.

Isla was the reason I got a Christmas tree. She was four and we went to Woolworths to buy decorations and then decorated the tree together. It became an annual tradition and we would make ornaments too. My brother Christopher has all the decorations I made for our parents' tree – papier-mâché baubles which I painted and embellished with sequins and feathers. When Isla and I went to Mexico, we brought back two papier-mâché dolls we called Blondie and Brownie, on account of their hair colour. I helped Isla make a Christmas outfit and the dolls take it in turns to wear it and sit on the top of the tree. In the interests of fairness every year we write on the box which doll has had an outing so we know whose turn it is the following year! Isla still comes over but now I use it as an excuse for an open house and invite family and friends to come to my flat and help me decorate the Christmas tree. There is wine and food and we unpack boxes of my vintage decorations that I have amassed over many years. I love the camaraderie of us all working together and now Isla's daughter, Jess, joins in – she is a similar age to what Isla was when she started the tradition.

I get together with all my family at some point over the festive season too, usually at my sister Fiona's house. She puts on a delicious buffet feast and the star dish is Anne's Chicken – which is of course chicken, in a Campbell's condensed soup sauce with a topping of crunched-up crisps. It was named after a friend of my parents who used to cook it for us so it's a nostalgic link to our childhood and we all take big spoonfuls. My siblings, nieces and their children are all there and we play games and have a tradition of watching *Dinner for One*, a black-and-white short film, based on a British sketch, filmed by a German broadcaster, which became customary viewing every New Year's Eve across a large proportion of Europe. I can't remember when or how we first discovered it but we watch it every year. The butler pretends to be serving long dead guests – he plays each of the guests – for the lady of the house and gets drunker as the meal progresses. It's a clever, witty sketch that makes us all laugh and it's only about 20 minutes long so ideal viewing.

As I mentioned before, I don't have a telly. I watch the occasional thing on my laptop and I like going to the cinema but I want to spend any spare time I have walking, reading and drawing more – I'm less detailed than in my youth and use gouache and crayons now. I go for long walks and stop to draw and paint when I'm away in Greece too, my spiritual home.

I went to Sifnos in Greece for the first time in 1985 with my friend Susie Slack and my then boyfriend Mervyn. They had been going since the late sixties and as soon as I got there, I could see why – I was hooked. We had the best times! Susie and I would make outfits out of cardboard and feathers, dress up in them and stage tableaux of Greek myths which we took photos of. There's a little shop that we nicknamed 'The Everything Shop' because that is exactly what it sells, everything (apart from food), including fabrics, clothes, religious tapestry kits, thread, pots and pans – a sort of hardware store. On one trip I had packed badly and forgotten to bring shirts with me so I popped to The Everything Shop and bought two fabrics – blue and red geometric and one with little people on it – and a traditional blue and white tape used on drawstring backpacks that the farmers had. I also bought poppers and thread and hand-sewed the two shirts, showing the stitches as a feature, using the tape as placket (an opening) and displaying the raw edge of binding around the neck. They were a bit of a 'roughly made' statement and I still wear them many years later although I don't chuck them in the washing machine, I handwash them just in case.

We always stayed with the same farming family and rented a house in their garden – a simply converted pigeon loft – which I still return to now. Their son was about eight when I first started going and we went to his wedding a few years ago, where we helped with the cooking and took part in several days of wonderful celebrations. I loved the rituals associated with the nuptials, like the special meals, the parties and the custom of rolling a baby on a bed covered in money! The music was exhilarating – Greek bands are such fun to dance to.

I go to Greece a couple of times a year if I can and always try to get there in spring. They have such amazing Easter celebrations that I really enjoy. Once there was a boy throwing bangers under the priest's garments and he shooed the boy away. There is also an annual 'Panigiri' – a summer festival where their saint is celebrated. The icon is sent from Athens (where it is kept) on a big boat and then transferred to a smaller boat to make its final journey to Chrissopighi – a rocky peninsula stretching out from Sifnos – and the Church of the Seven Martyrs. The icon is carried up the steps as people reach out to touch and kiss it and then it goes on a procession around the island, visiting the sick and elderly, before it ends up at the beautiful whitewashed church for a big ceremony. I try to catch this every year.

There were so many things I missed about Sifnos when

we couldn't travel during the pandemic. I can walk for miles there and, depending what time of year it is, I eat ripe figs straight from the trees or sweet juicy mulberries. I pick lots of herbs too and tie them in bunches, hanging them outside to dry in the sun. Thyme buds are delicious and not available in the UK so I always bring some back and store them in jars, as well as capers in salt.

I have another interest which may sound a little macabre: I collect skeletons, specifically the skulls of dead animals. If I find one, I boil it to disinfect it, wrap it up and bring it home with me. A chef gave me a boar's head and I have a ram's head, a sheep's head and a snake's backbone on my shelf. I really like how they look and am fascinated by structure. I draw them too. My sketchbook is always out in Greece and I will stop to draw and paint scenes, wild flowers and objects that are inside the house. I love the freedom and discovery of Sifnos but I feel like that about London too. I'm hoping to return soon with Isla, who often comes with me, and this time her daughter Jess too.

I feel no different from the girl who plunged headfirst into the fashion industry half a century ago. I'm still the same – I continue to search out new challenges, listen more than I talk, learn something every day and spend time with the people who matter. Fame doesn't interest me and never has, whether it's other people or myself. It's nice meeting people when I'm out and about, who have enjoyed the *Sewing Bee* and want to talk about it.

I always stop and have a chat, or do a selfie if they want one. One day, I was walking down the road and Grayson Perry, riding on his bike, saw me and stopped for a chat. Someone walking behind me saw Grayson and asked if they could have a selfie, so Grayson said, 'Do you want me, or her?' pointing at me. I turned round and they said, 'Ooh, can I have both of you?'

My sister Fiona and my brother Jeremy are keen on opera and so I quite often get invited to the English National Opera – happily, I am Jeremy's first port of call if he has anyone cancel. I was there with Jeremy and Kate one evening and Jeremy spotted a friend of his, Murray, who is on the ENO music staff. He went over and had a chat, then Murray said, 'The person sitting next to you, is that Esme from the *Sewing Bee*? I'm a big *Sewing Bee* fan.'

'Yes, it is,' said Jeremy.

'How do you know her?' he asked.

'Well, she's my sister,' Jeremy replied. 'Come over and say hello.'

We had a nice chat and he was very charming.

⊗ ⊗ ⊗

Another trip to the ENO, a matinee, was followed by dinner with a big group of friends, then someone suggested we went to the Ivy Club for a drink. The only man who came with us was Jeremy, the rest of the men went home because they were too tired. Then my friend Barbara, who had membership to Ronnie Scotts, suggested we go on there.

So we went to Upstairs at Ronnie Scotts and I immediately hit the dance floor. The youngsters, even Helen who is 40 years younger than me, had all gone by 1:30, but I kept dancing until the end and got home at about 4am – I do love to dance and the kids have no stamina these days!

I'm on Instagram now but social media is still a mystery to me and it feels a bit like showing off. In my day we got on with our work, plying our trade – we didn't spend time shouting about it or taking lots of photos of us with celebrities. Of course, things have changed now but I'm old school about privacy. That might sound hypocritical as I have delved into my life and shared it with you here in this book, but I hope my message throughout has been to plough your own furrow and not be distracted by the noise and fuss of what others are doing.

When I think about the themes that run through my life and what is important to me, there are some common threads throughout. Of course, one is sewing, which has led me to so many new places and exciting adventures – who would have thought? But there are others too.

I have always followed my dreams and I think everyone should if they have the opportunity. My dreams have always been about creativity, art and fashion, but I'm also always up for trying new things and being open to new opportunities and adventures. Go on television at 70? Sure, why not? Don't underestimate yourself, have a go – after all, how bad can it be?

Another element is collaboration and working with

others. I have always enjoyed working as part of a group, from the true collective that was Swanky Modes to the hundreds of skills and activities that go to make up a film or television programme. Part of that is being helpful and kind and supporting and encouraging those around you. You can always learn from those around you, whether they are the 'experts' in the field, or the beginners learning their skills. The naïve approach from an absolute beginner sometimes uncovers an innovative technique, or creates something entirely new. It's about respecting people and seeing what they may be able to contribute – sometimes you'll be surprised.

And sometimes you may get something in return. So often in my career I have gone on to work with, or for, those who once worked for me. Much of my film work came from the talented people who had done placements at Swanky Modes and then called me up when they needed some help with films or adverts. My teaching career came the same way, as did my collaboration with Ashish Gupta. More importantly though, this is how I have made many of my lifelong friends, and friends and family are such an important part of my life.

You may have spotted another theme – that I love to party, particularly if there is dancing involved. Enjoy yourself and have fun, at work or play.

And finally, appreciate what you have. I have never really been focused on money as an end in itself but I realise how lucky I am to have been born when and where

I was, with the opportunities that I have had. So many people in the world are not as lucky.

When my publishing editor talked about the cover of this book I asked if we could do the shoot in my studio. Natalie was there the day they came and thought it was brilliant that there was a make-up artist and hairdresser just for me, considering we usually work behind the scenes. She said wasn't it funny how life changes but how I was still exactly the same, totally and utterly myself? And I said, 'This is who I am. I can't pretend to be anyone else at this stage of my life. I can only be me.'

Filmography

FILMS I HAVE WORKED ON INCLUDE:

Saint-Ex (Director Anand Tucker) 1996, outfits for Miranda Richardson and Janet McTeer

Trainspotting (Danny Boyle) 1996, Dale Winton's pink lurex suit and his assistant's dress

Fierce Creatures (Fred Schepisi, Robert Young) 1997, Jamie Lee Curtis

Wonderland (Michael Winterbottom) 1999

The Beach (Danny Boyle) 2000, outfits for Leonardo DiCaprio and Tilda Swinton

Bridget Jones's Diary (Sharon Maguire) 2001, Renee Zellweger's bunny outfit, the skirt at the fire station and Honor Blackman's outfit

Captain Corelli's Mandolin (John Madden) 2001

28 Days Later (Danny Boyle) 2002

24 Hour Party People (Michael Winterbottom) 2002, outfits for Steve Coogan

Heartlands (Damien O'Donnell) 2002

Code 46 (Michael Winterbottom) 2003

Agent Cody Banks (Harold Zwart) 2003, made the girls' DJs and the African rulers outfit

Derailed (Mikael Hafstrom) 2005

Breaking and Entering (Anthony Mingella) 2006, made outfits for Juliette Binoche

1408 (Mikael Hafstrom) 2007, made John Cusack's shirts

Last Chance Harvey (Joel Hopkins) 2008, outfits for Emma Thompson

The Boy in the Striped Pyjamas (Mark Herman) 2008

Is Anybody There? (John Crowley) 2008

The Debt (John Madden) 2010

Never Let Me Go (Mark Romanek) 2010, outfits for Carey Mulligan and Charlotte Rampling

Wuthering Heights (Andrea Arnold) 2011, young Cathy outfits

Appropriate Adult (Julian Jarrold) 2011, outfits for Emily Watson

Le Weekend (Roger Michell) 2013, Lindsey Duncan

Under the Skin (Jonathan Glazer) 2013

The Riot Club (Lone Scherfig) 2014

Black Sea (Kevin MacDonald) 2014, Jude Law's shirts

Two Faces of January (Hossein Amini) 2014, Kirsten
Dunst's outfits

A Monster Calls (JA Bayona) 2016, outfits for Felicity
Jones and Sigourney Weaver

Bridget Jones's Baby (Sharon Maguire) 2016, outfits for
Renee Zellwegger

Trainspotting 2 (Danny Boyle) 2017, outfits for Anjela
Nedyalkova

The Little Stranger (Lenny Abrahamson) 2018, outfits
for Ruth Wilson

Acknowledgements

I'm a natural storyteller but my memory can slow me down so I talked to a merry band of family and friends to help in the writing of this book. Not only am I grateful for their input but also for them generously allowing me to share stories that belong as much to them as they do to me. This experience has turned out to be happily nostalgic and a lot of fun.

My first debt of gratitude goes to my publisher, Bonnier Books, especially Susannah Otter and Madiya Altaf for inviting me to write this book in the first place and for their dedication and support throughout. The same to Lucy Brazier for being on this journey with me and to my brilliant agent, Matt Nicholls at United Agents.

Huge thanks to my fellow Swanky Modes colleagues and lifelong friends, Willie Walters, Judy Dewsbury and Melanie

Langer. The book gave us an excuse for a long, boozy Soho lunch – not that we need much encouragement – and their collective memories were invaluable. Additional appreciation to Anne Martin, Niall McInerney, John Grant, Cynthia Lole, Tamsin Walters, Isla Wickham and Ben Haberfield for adding such colour and vibrancy to the page.

To Steven Noble, Rachael Fleming, Natalie Ward and Liza Bracey who have been colleagues and mates for more years than we care to admit and continue to make me hoot with laughter, thank you for sharing your memories. And to Annabel Hodin, for reminding me of stories I didn't want to forget.

The Great British Sewing Bee is a team of dreams but I want to give a special shout out to Susanne Rock and Patrick Grant for their thoughts and to Joe Lycett for recounting the funniest stories. The next round is on me, Joe!

To everyone at Central Saint Martins but specifically to Natalie Gibson, Louis Loizou, Patrick Lee Yow, Alistair O'Neill and Ashish Gupta for giving your valuable time and filling in the gaps so beautifully.

Finally, to my family. To my parents, who are very much a part of who I am. The first two chapters of the book focus on my childhood and my siblings – Fiona, Christopher, Angus and Jeremy. My wholehearted thanks to them for supporting me throughout this book-writing process, for their additions, corrections and reminders and for being so open about their own early lives. Particularly Christopher and Jeremy for their forensic care and attention to the book.